THE CHOCOLATE COOKBOOK

Also by Juliette Elkon

THE BELGIAN WAR RELIEF COOKBOOK

THE HONEY COOKBOOK

A BELGIAN COOKBOOK

THE BELGIAN CALENDAR BOOK OF RECIPES

MENUS FOR ENTERTAINING
(with Elaine Ross)

BY

Juliette Elkon Hamelecourt

A Bobbs-Merrill Book

MACMILLAN PUBLISHING COMPANY
New York

Macmillan Publishing Company
866 Third Avenue, New York, N.Y. 10022
Collier Macmillan Canada, Inc.

Library of Congress Cataloging-in-Publication Data

Hamelecourt, Juliette Elkon.
  The chocolate cookbook.

  "A Bobbs-Merrill book."
  Includes index.
  1. Cookery (Chocolate) I. Title.
TX767.C5H26   1985   641.6'374   85-18964
ISBN 0-02-535270-9

Macmillan books are available at special discounts for bulk purchases for sales promotions, premiums, fund-raising, or educational use. For details, contact:

    Special Sales Director
    Macmillan Publishing Company
    866 Third Avenue
    New York, N.Y. 10022

10 9 8 7 6 5 4 3 2 1

Printed in the United States of America

Dedicated to my children
Jacqueline, Babette, and Peter
The greedy tasters

Acknowledgments

For providing background information my sincere thanks go to Irma Hyams of the Chocolate Information Council; Eleanor B. Sloan, Supervisor of the Test Kitchens, Hershey Foods Corporation; Janet Oberndorfer, formerly of the Wheat Flour Institute; Katherine C. Egan, General Foods Kitchen Baker's Products; Louise J. Whitaker, Flavor and Extract Manufacturers' Association; Helen J. Britt, Director, Home Economics and Consumer Service, Nestlé Company; The California Almond Growers Exchange; The National Egg Council; Sugar Information, Inc.; and The Dairy Council of Metropolitan New York.

For chasing dangling participles across the pages and tirelessly checking and rechecking recipes, my fond thanks to Alice Tibbetts and Hugh Ferrell.

Contents

Introduction

When the Spanish landed in Mexico, Atauchi, Montezuma's brother, went to meet Cortez and his soldiers, taking with him llamas, guacacos, vicunas, alpacas, stags, roe deer, deer, rabbits, partridges, loads of dried meat, loads of *chocolate loaves,* corn in both grain and meal form, quantities of fruit, both fresh and dried, honey in pots and in the comb, resin chicle, and all sorts of animals peculiar to the region. The Spaniards were led to lodgings decorated with flowers and sweet-smelling branches and given their first taste of *Xocolatl,* or, as the interpreter explained, "Sour Water."

Montezuma then received Cortez at his palace. They sat down on solid gold stools while courtiers and retainers watched the proceedings. Court musicians chanted and danced and recited poetry. For the feast, the Inca had exacted from lesser kings twenty chests of ground chocolate beans and maize, two thousand loaves of very white salt, molded, and eighty loaves of red chocolate, or chocolate which had been heated to liquefy the cocoa butter, then molded in a process which was not too far removed from the contemporary principles of chocolate manufacture.

Curious about this beverage *Xocolatl,* the Spaniards made inquiries and were taken to see the cocoa tree, which was later to be named by

Linnaeus *theobroma cocoa,* "The godly drink cocoa tree." They saw frail trees, almost rootless, reputed to be thirty to fifty years old, growing densely together in the shade of larger trees, some reaching sixty feet high. The tree trunks and the branches were hung with balloonlike pods, some purple with variegated flecks, others maroon, green, or brown. White-clad pickers placed the pods in large earthen crocks, which were carried away by slaves to a place where breakers, armed with obsidian knives, split the shells.

Women and children scooped out the cream-colored beans, which turned purple after exposure to air. But most of the beans, piled in baskets, were allowed to ferment, to generate their own heat, a process which we now know brought out the essential oils of chocolate by converting its natural sugars to acetic acid.

After fermentation the beans or *nibs* were sun-dried, roasted lightly to remove the last shell, and finally pounded in a large mortar until, because of their heavy fat content and the heat, the beans turned to a paste. The paste was shaped into small loaves the size of a fist, then wrapped in maize leaves and tied with dried grasses.

To make *Xocolatl* the loaves were unwrapped, grated, and melted in a thin, lightly salted cornmush. The narrow clay pots into which it was poured had a perforated lid into which a hardwood rotary beater or *molinillo* was inserted. Rubbed between the palms of the hands, this beater emulsified the beverage and produced a froth. According to one authority, Montezuma took snow from the heights of a nearby volcano and poured whipped *Xocolatl* over it—result: chocolate ice.

Needless to say, cocoa beans, chocolate loaves, chocolate pots with their *molinillos,* and tall cups were part of the first cargoes to Spain. Cortez wrote to Spain, *"Una taza de este precioso brebaje permete un hombre de andar un dia entero sin tomar alimente."* ("A cup of this precious beverage permits a man to walk an entire day without food.")

There was much interest in *Xocolatl* at the Spanish court. The king and queen drank it regularly, and although court authors confess no one really liked it, everyone felt obliged to pretend. Among the circle of court intimates, however, there was a certain rambunctious duchess secure enough in wealth and position to dare express the opinion that the Mexican drink tasted bitter. She set about to improve its flavor with sugar and presented the queen with a *creamy* chocolate. Soon this improved chocolate was sipped by everyone and poured from individual silver pots into silver goblets copied from the terra cotta goblets of the Indians. The ladies-in-waiting vied with each other to compose the most perfect blend of spices to flavor the beverage. Taste for spices was heavy and we shudder to think that as much as a pinch of mace went into one cup with a pinch of cinnamon. Someone else added vanilla and served it hot.

Chocolate traveled to France with the Spanish bride of Louis XIV, and to the Low Countries with the Duke of Alba. Of Queen Marie-Thérèse, the Duke of St. Simon says in his memoir that she thought nothing of downing two formal meals a day and still drank her six to seven cups of frothy chocolate in her own apartments among her retinue of Spanish cardinals and ladies-in-waiting.

With the craze for chocolate came the craze for chocolate pots and chocolate cups. The silversmiths of France and Italy, the porcelain manufacturers of Sèvres, Rouen, Strasbourg, Creil, and Brussels made *chocolatières* as impressive in craftsmanship as in price. Many of the rare and more precious examples of chocolate serving pieces are now exhibited in museums. Mme. de Pompadour owned the most expensive porcelain set ever made, one of the many ordered in China and brought back by the merchants of the Compagnie des Indes. For elaborate designs, the baroque art of the Austrian court outdid every other, and the Austrian chocolate sets are as rich as their desserts.

As the flavor of hot chocolate became more and more adapted to European taste, its use became generalized. In 1657 there appeared the first of many English Chocolate Houses where ladies and gentlemen stopped every day to enjoy a cup of Spanish chocolate. Nearly all great gourmets of the time experimented with chocolate confections, but the true genius was César Gabriel Choiseul, duc de Praslin, who fathered the praline.

Secretary of the Navy under Louis XV of France, he was the proprietor of large plantations in the north of Haiti; his daughter received a concession to the island of Tortuga. From their plantations came cashews, chocolate, vanilla, brown sugar, and beautiful tawny rum. César Gabriel poured caramel over his cashews and pounded the brittle into a fine powder which is still known today as *Poudre de Praslin*. He melted vanilla-flavored chocolate with rum. To it he added sweet butter until it was creamy. When cool he mixed in enough of his powdered brittle to give the chocolate the consistency necessary for rolling it into the shape of a truffle. He dusted the black gems with sugar, cocoa, and cinnamon and delighted his friends. All the variations of creole pralines with or without chocolate are imitations of this.

French confectioners, however, did not have cashews to work with, and soon the original nuts were replaced by the more easily procurable hazelnut. The hand methods of manufacture used by small *chocolatiers* gave way in time to mass production. The transition was hastened by the advent of a perfected steam engine capable of handling the cacao grinding process. By 1730 chocolate had dropped in price from three dollars a pound to the financial reach of others besides the very wealthy. The cocoa press invented in 1828 did much more to cut prices and helped to improve the quality of the beverage by squeezing out part of the cocoa butter. Drinking chocolate now had more of the smooth consistency and pleasing flavor that it has today. It was in pre-revolutionary New England in 1765 that the first chocolate factory was established.

The nineteenth century was marked by two additional revolutionary developments in the history of chocolate. In 1876, Daniel Peter in Vevey, Switzerland, invented a way of making milk chocolate bars for eating. Filled with fondant, they became a gourmet's delight.

Today, world production of cocoa beans is currently estimated at 850,000 tons, with Ghana as leader; Brazil, Nigeria, the Cameroons, Ivory Coast, the Dominican Republic, Ecuador, Venezuela, Mexico, Colombia, and Haiti are lesser but important producers.

The Western Hemisphere, the original home of the cocoa bean, does not now produce enough to meet the demands of its own nations. The biggest supplier on this side of the Atlantic is Brazil. The United States is the largest consumer of chocolate and chocolate products.

What Queen Marie-Thérèse's Dr. Bachot said of it in 1685 still holds true: "Well-made chocolate is such a noble invention that it, rather than nectar and ambrosia, should be known as the food of the gods."

Chocolate Information

Commercial chocolate comes in many forms, but not all chocolate foods are real chocolate. The food and drug ordinances do not protect us from substitutions of artificial flavoring. Read labels.

Real chocolate, real vanilla, real butter, real flavorings in general are what you should look for in packaged or baked chocolate goods, and what you should use when you bake your own.

Cocoa beans: Source of all chocolate and cocoa, cocoa beans are found in the pods (fruit) of the cocoa tree, an evergreen cultivated mainly within twenty degrees north or south of the equator.

Nibs: Nibs are the "meat" of the cocoa bean.

Chocolate liquid: Sometimes called "chocolate liquor," the base material of all chocolate and cocoa products comes from ground nibs.

Cocoa butter: The yellowish-white vegetable fat, removed from chocolate liquid under high pressure.

Bitter or unsweetened chocolate: Chocolate liquid which has been cooled and molded into blocks, the best for baking or cooking.

Semisweet and sweet chocolate: Prepared by blending chocolate liquid with varying amounts of sweetening and added cocoa butter. Flavorings may be included. After processing, the chocolate is cooled. Sweet chocolate is usually molded into bars. Semisweet chocolate is also available in bar form, but most popularly as pieces. This is the generic term. Different manufacturers use different names such as *blocs, squares, bits,* etc. Chocolate is also granulated and known as "shot," used for decoration by candy makers and confectioners.

Milk chocolate: The best known kind of eating chocolate. Milk chocolate is made by combining the chocolate liquid, extra cocoa butter, milk or cream, sweetening, and flavorings.

Cocoa powder: General term for the portion of chocolate liquid that remains after most of the cocoa butter has been removed. The term includes breakfast cocoa, medium and low fat cocoas, and Dutch process cocoa.

Breakfast cocoa: Cocoa powder with at least twenty-two percent cocoa butter.

Medium fat cocoa: Cocoa powder containing between ten and twenty-two percent cocoa butter.

Low fat cocoa: Cocoa powder containing less than ten percent cocoa butter.

Dutch process cocoa: Cocoa powder which has been treated with alkali to neutralize the natural acids; darker in color and slightly different in flavor from natural cocoa.

5

Ready to use cocoa: Mixture of cocoa powder, sweetening, and other flavorings.

Chocolate syrup: Combination of chocolate or cocoa flavoring, sweetening, water, salt, and other flavorings.

Chocolate sauce: Essentially the same as chocolate syrup, but heavier in density resulting from the addition of milk, cream, and/or butter.

White chocolate: A substance erroneously called chocolate since it contains no chocolate liquid and therefore does not comply with government standards for chocolate. Actually "confectioners' " coating, it is sometimes made with vegetable fats instead of cocoa butter, tinted with vegetable coloring, and contains added flavors.

When a product boasts real chocolate flavor, check the label. The word "flavor" is a giveaway. Is it made from cocoa or chocolate, or is there no chocolate at all, only artificial coloring and artificial flavors?

Check again: ground spices, ground vanilla beans, oleoresin or extract, or natural food oils, salt, ground coffee, ground nut meats, and dried malted cereal extracts are natural flavorings. When the chocolate is flavored with any of these ingredients, the label will state, "spiced," "spice added," "flavored with (specifically naming the ingredients)," "with added flavoring" (unspecified if a production secret is to be guarded), or "with added _____" (the blank being filled in with the specific common name of the flavoring used). Learn to understand the labels if you want real chocolate and real flavorings.

The word "alkali" on a label is a chemical term for some form or other of soda—perfectly harmless in the quantities used.

"Lecithin" is also a natural substance containing glycerophosphoric acid needed for your daily diet. It is used as an *emulsifier*.

Natural sweeteners are sugar, dried corn syrup, dextrose, or glucose syrup. Artificial sweeteners should be used only on medical recommendation. They cannot replace the many functions that sugar performs.

Vegetable fat means fat other than cocoa, but otherwise just what it says —oil, stearin, or a combination which has a melting point higher than cocoa fat and makes a better-looking product.

Storing: Always store chocolate in a cool (never higher than 78° temperature), dry place. When the storage place is too hot, the cocoa butter in the chocolate softens and rises to the surface, where it forms a gray film known as "bloom." Chocolate with bloom is safe to eat but may not taste as creamy. Use it for baking or in sauces.

Milk chocolate, particularly, absorbs flavors and odors of other foods; wrap very tightly.

All chocolate may be refrigerated, but again, be sure to wrap well so it doesn't absorb refrigerator odors. Chocolate, when refrigerated, becomes very brittle. Chocolate may be frozen for as long as three to four months without change in flavor, texture, or appearance.

Cocoa: Best conditions for storing cocoa are at temperatures of 60–70° and at 50–65 percent relative humidity. Cocoa tends to lump and lose its rich brown color if exposed to high temperature or humidity. Flavor is not affected but the cocoa looks less appetizing. Cocoa should always be stored in a tightly sealed container.

Substitutions

It's better to use the type of chocolate or cocoa your recipe specifies, since each has its own special properties. If you *must* substitute, follow the equivalents given here to be on the safe side.

Semisweet chocolate: One square (1 oz.) of any sweet cooking or semisweet chocolate can be used interchangeably with 1 ounce chocolate pieces.

Cocoa: Because cocoa tends to thicken more than chocolate and therefore makes a stronger flavor, to substitute cocoa for chocolate in beverages, use only ⅔ as much cocoa by weight, or 3 to 3½ tablespoons for each ounce of chocolate called for.

To substitute cocoa for chocolate, use 3 tablespoons cocoa plus 1 tablespoon of any fat substance in recipes that call for 1 ounce of chocolate.

For chocolate fanciers who develop allergies, carob flour, milled from St. John's bread or tamarind, may be used in the cocoa recipes in this book by doubling cocoa quantities in the recipes. Carob scorches easily—temperatures have to be adjusted to no higher than 300°. Consequently baking will require approximately 5 minutes longer per 25°. When substituting carob for chocolate in the chocolate recipes, you will have to experiment because it doesn't always work, although some people claim good results.

Preparing Chocolate

Melting: Chocolate can be melted either dry (over simmering water in a double boiler) or in liquid. Either way, use low heat since chocolate scorches easily. Always cool the melted chocolate gradually.

Dry melting: Have bowl, spoon, or spatula absolutely dry. (Stir chocolate often for smooth, even consistency.) Cook over hot but not boiling water to be certain there is no rising steam. If even a drop of condensed moisture falls into the melting chocolate it will stiffen and be almost impossible to use. However, if this should happen, you can rescue the chocolate. Stir in 1 to 2 tablespoons of corn or peanut oil (*not* butter, since it contains moisture) until chocolate becomes fluid again. To melt a small quantity—1 to 2 ounces—wrap chocolate in aluminum foil and place in a *warm* spot on the stove, over the pilot, for example.

Melting in liquid: Use ¼ cup liquid—juice, water, spirits—to 6 ounces of chocolate, and melt over direct low heat. Stir constantly so melting chocolate and liquid blend thoroughly. When adding liquids to melted chocolate, be sure to add 2 or more tablespoons of the liquid at a time; otherwise the chocolate will stiffen and will not blend.

To curl: Use a vegetable peeler with a long narrow blade. Warm chocolate and blade slightly. Draw peeler along smooth surface of a chunk or bar of chocolate. For large curls pull peeler over wide surface of chocolate; for small ones, pull blade along narrow side.

To grate: Chocolate must be cool and firm. Grate on hand grater or rotary type with hand crank. Clean often so chocolate doesn't clog grating surface. A blender can also be used, but then be sure to cut chocolate in small pieces.

To chop: Place on wooden cutting board and use a sharp, heavy knife or cleaver. Chopped chocolate should be about the size of a pea.

Chocolate may be grated, curled, or chopped for decorative purposes as well as for cooking or to speed up melting. Whatever the process or purpose, here are a few basic rules to follow for best results:

1. Handle the chocolate as little as possible.
2. Be sure your implements are absolutely dry.
3. If not using immediately, refrigerate the chocolate to prevent its lumping together.

Nuts

Nuts and chocolate are made for each other. Nuts can be bought slivered, diced, sliced, or blanched.

To preserve freshness, keep the shelled nuts in a tightly closed container in the refrigerator or in the freezer. Shelled nuts have their brown skins left on. Blanched nuts are those from which the skins have been removed. To blanch, cover the shelled nuts with water and bring to a boil. Drain. The skins will slip off easily when the nut is pressed between thumb and fingers.

Roasting or toasting enhances the flavor of all nuts. To roast, use 1 teaspoon of butter or oil for each cup of nutmeats. Roast for 15 to 20 minutes, stirring frequently, in a 300° oven. To toast nuts, place kernels in a 300° (slow) oven for 15 to 20 minutes until golden brown, stirring occasionally.

Chopping roasted nuts is easier when they have just come out of the oven.

Almonds should be slivered when the blanched kernels are still warm and moist. Split each nut in half with the tip of a knife; lay flat side down and slice into thin slivers.

Candied Fruit

Candied fruit has been glazed in syrup and will "weep" and spoil if refrigerated. To store, place in a tight-lidded jar in a cool dry place. Raisins, prunes, dried dates and figs should be bagged in polyethylene and stored in the refrigerator to keep moist.

Baking Information

Stone-ground natural flour, which is not enriched because nothing has been removed from it, is available only at health-food counters. It is expensive but worthwhile. It can be used in place of all-purpose flour in any recipe in this book.

All-purpose flour, sometimes called general purpose or family flour, is most commonly used for home baking. It is packed in two-, five-, or ten-pound sacks and is always enriched with the B-vitamins—thiamine, niacin, and riboflavin—and the mineral, iron.

Self-rising flours are all-purpose flours to which leavening and salt have been added. The leavening agents used are sodium bicarbonate and acid-reacting substances such as monocalcium phosphate, sodium acid pyrophosphate, sodium aluminum phosphate, or a combination of these acids.

The sodium bicarbonate and the acid ingredient react in the presence of liquid to release harmless carbon dioxide. In home baking equivalents, the amounts of leavening added are 1½ teaspoons per cup of flour. Self-rising flour may be used interchangeably with all-purpose flour by omitting the baking powder and salt called for in most recipes. Self-rising flour is not recommended for popovers or egg-leavened cakes, because excess leavening will cause an overrise and then a collapse.

Phosphated flour is all-purpose flour to which the acid-reacting ingredient monocalcium phosphate has been added in a quantity of not more than 0.75 percent of the weight of the finished phosphated flour. It helps stabilize gluten and helps nourish yeast, which cannot live without phosphates. It is used mostly in the southeastern United States.

Cake flours are milled from low protein soft wheat particularly suitable for baking cakes and pastries. Cake flours are usually not enriched, but they are bleached to remove the natural pigment for commercial reasons only. The buyer has been programmed to choose white flour. Commercially bleached flours contain toxic substances such as benzoyl peroxide, chlorine dioxide, or chlorine to remove the pigment quickly and eliminate costly storage for the manufacturer. Pastry flours are never bleached.

Instantized, instant blending, or quick mixing flour pours like salt right through a screen or sieve. It blends instantly in cold liquid without lumping. This new flour is all-purpose, although it requires about one-fourth more liquid in a recipe. It may be used in almost all recipes in place of regular flour.

Leavening and rising. The cellular structure of baked goods is leavened or made light and porous by internal pressure or expansion. Tiny air pockets form in the gluten cells, causing the walls to stretch. Beating the batter, adding beaten eggs, creaming sugar or fat, sifting flour, all incorporate air into the batter. The heat converts part of the liquid ingredients to steam within the cells of a cake dough or batter, causing it to rise again when baked.

Active dry yeast is a dehydrated form of compressed yeast from which approximately ninety-two percent of the moisture has been removed. The yeast cells resume their activity when rehydrated in warm water, 105–115°. One cake of compressed yeast equals one envelope of active dry yeast. Under refrigeration, compressed yeast will keep one or two weeks. It may turn slightly brown but is still active if it crumbles between the fingers. Before use it should be softened in water a little cooler than that used to soften dry yeast, about 95°. Yeast gives a special, characteristic flavor, besides being a leavening agent.

Baking soda or sodium bicarbonate was the first of the chemical leaveners. When it reacts with an acid, harmless carbon dioxide is produced. The acid most frequently used is that contained in sour milk, sour cream, or buttermilk. Occasionally fruit juice, molasses, honey, or corn syrup provides the acid ingredient.

Baking powder, another leavener, contains tartaric acid or a combination of cream of tartar and tartaric acid. This type of baking powder is sometimes called "quick-acting," because its carbon dioxide is released as soon as it is combined with liquid and the reaction is completed at room temperature.

Phosphate baking powder usually employs monocalcium phosphate as the acid ingredient. About two-thirds of the carbon dioxide is released at room temperature and the remainder when the mixture is heated. Thus phosphate baking powders work more slowly than tartrate powders.

"Double-acting" or combination baking powders contain phosphate and tartaric acid, which react at different temperatures.

Measuring flour for baking. The standards for dry and liquid measurement in family size recipes in the United States are the cup, the tablespoon, the teaspoon, and their fractions. In Europe the ingredients are weighed. This is the more exact measure. Flour tends to compact in a measuring cup. This is why flour must sometimes be sifted several times. Use great care in measuring—do not rap or jar the cup.

Sugar. The total sugars of a dough or a batter are contained in the flour, the milk, and those added separately, such as sugar, molasses, syrups, and honey. Their primary function is to support fermentation or leavening.

Accurate mixing and beating make the dough or batter smooth, make it rise evenly, and give it a beautiful texture.

Baking time varies with each recipe according to the ingredients, their proportion, and the oven temperature. The interval between mixing and baking also influences the final result. Unless otherwise specified in a recipe, baking should be done as soon as the dough or batter is finished. This is why the oven should always be preheated. Its temperature should be accurate. If you have any doubts, place a small oven thermometer—available at all hardware stores—in the middle of the oven and check to see that it registers the same temperature as the stove thermostat. Inaccurate thermostats may be replaced upon request to the stove makers by sending the serial number of the stove. When I was a child in Belgium my grandmother tested oven heat by determining whether her naked forearm would be scorched in the oven. That was a signal to cover the coals with ashes to reduce the heat.

The process of baking is actually accomplished by all moisture being vaporized in the interior of the dough or batter when it reaches the boiling point. The rate at which this point is reached varies with each recipe. Biscuits, breads, cakes, and muffins must not reach internal temperatures above the boiling point. Waffles, cookies, and crackers require temperatures high enough to evaporate moisture quickly so that they become crisp.

The three ways of mixing fat into a batter—beating, creaming, and cutting in—make batters lighter. Cutting in, as is done in biscuit and pie doughs, blends the fat so that the result is a flaky or layered texture.

Eggs. As egg white is beaten, part of its protein coagulates; air is incorporated and volume increases. Chemically, egg whites are tricky and should be beaten exactly as written in the recipe. Holding a glossy peak means that the foam is shiny. Beating beyond this point breaks down the foam structure so that liquid drains to the bottom. Minimal beating, which is sometimes called for, helps leavening when certain ingredients are called for. Whisks are better than beaters because they incorporate more air. Egg whites whipped at room temperature attain more volume than those whipped at refrigerator temperature. Sugar should be added to the whites after foaming has started—it makes the foam more stable. Cream of tartar, acetic acid, and citric acid also help.

Egg yolk will form a moderate foam when beaten; whole eggs behave more like the yolk than like the white. Even a drop of yolk will prevent white from foaming satisfactorily.

Milk. If, instead of whole milk, you wish to use: *Skim milk,* add ½ teaspoon sweet butter per cup. *Dry powdered skim milk* when made according to package directions is the same as fresh skim milk and may be treated the same way. *Evaporated milk,* dilute with an equal amount of water. *Condensed milk* contains 40 to 45 percent sugar. Dilute according to directions and omit ⅔ of the sugar in the recipe. To make 1 cup of sour milk, add 1 slice of lemon and let it curdle. Use whenever called for in a recipe.

The best eggs for baking are medium grade A. Butter and margarine may be used interchangeably as well as solid vegetable shortenings.

Cakes

Devil's Food Cake

Preheat oven to 350°.
Mix:

> ¾ cup boiling water
> 3 ounces grated unsweetened chocolate

and cook over hot, but not boiling, water, uncovered, until thick and smooth.
Cool. Reserve. Cream:

> ¾ cup salted butter

Gradually add:

> 1½ cups granulated sugar

beating until light and fluffy. Add one at a time:

> 3 eggs

beating 1 minute after each addition. Blend in the cooled chocolate mixture.

Sift together:

> 2½ cups cake flour
> 1½ teaspoons soda
> ¾ teaspoon salt

Add the dry ingredients alternately with:

> ¾ cup buttermilk

Add:

> 1 teaspoon vanilla

Pour into 2 greased and floured 9-inch round layer pans. Bake for 30 to 35 minutes.

Fill and frost with any of the following:

FILLINGS:

Chocolate Fudge, page 65

Prune and Nut, page 75

Apricot Jam

Orange Topping, page 72

Minted Topping, page 74

FROSTINGS:

Chocolate Fudge, page 65

Rich Chocolate, page 68

Chocolate Italian Meringue, page 59

Chocolate Marshmallow, page 68

Minted Topping, page 74

Double Chocolate Cake

Preheat oven to 350°.

Beat until thick and lemon-colored:

> 2 eggs

Add gradually:

> 1¼ cups sugar

and beat until well blended.
Sift together:

> 1½ cups sifted all-purpose flour
> 1¼ teaspoons soda
> 1 teaspoon salt
> ½ cup cocoa

Add:

> ⅔ cup vegetable oil
> 1 cup buttermilk
> 1 teaspoon vanilla

Beat until smooth. Fold in egg mixture. Pour into 8-inch layer pans greased on the bottom and lined with waxed paper. Bake 35 to 40 minutes, or until done.

FILLINGS:

Raspberry Jam
Cherry Topping, page 74
Blended Mocha Butter Cream, page 70
Blended Chocolate Butter Cream, page 71

FROSTINGS:

Instant Frosting, page 66
Chocolate Marshmallow Icing, page 60
Blended Mocha Butter Cream, page 70
Blended Chocolate Butter Cream, page 71

Cocoa Cake

Preheat oven to 350°.
Cream until light and fluffy:

> 1 cup sweet butter or margarine
> 2¼ cups sugar

Add, one at a time, beating well after each addition:

> 2 eggs

Add:

> 1 teaspoon vanilla

Sift together:

> ½ cup cocoa
> 3 cups sifted cake flour
> 2 teaspoons baking soda
> 1 teaspoon salt

Add to creamed mixture alternately with:

> 2 cups buttermilk

beginning and ending with dry ingredients. Pour into greased and floured pans. Bake as follows:

3 9-inch layer pans	30 to 35 minutes
1 13×9×2¼-inch pan	55 to 60 minutes

Fill and frost with:

> Instant Frosting, page 66, or
> Cocoa Fudge Frosting, page 65

Saucepan Fudge Cake

Preheat oven to 350°.
In a saucepan over low heat melt:

> 2 ounces unsweetened chocolate
> 2 tablespoons salted butter

Add:

> ⅓ cup water
> ½ cup granulated sugar

Stir until the sugar is dissolved.
Remove from the heat and stir in:

> ½ cup light corn syrup

Cool to room temperature.
Meanwhile, sift:

> 1 cup all-purpose flour
> ½ teaspoon salt
> ½ teaspoon baking powder
> 1 teaspoon baking soda

and sift again. Add:

>1 egg

to the cooled chocolate mixture and mix well. Add the dry ingredients and stir until well blended. Add:

>¼ cup buttermilk
>1 teaspoon vanilla extract

Blend thoroughly. Pour the batter into a greased and floured 8×8×2-inch square pan. Bake for 30 to 35 minutes or until done. Serve warm with ice cream or:

>**Chocolate Cinnamon-Flecked Topping, page 74**

Brownstone Cake

An Old American cake.

Preheat oven to 325°.
Dissolve:

>**2 ounces unsweetened chocolate in**
>**1 cup hot water**

Cool. Sift together over waxed paper:

>**2 cups all-purpose flour**
>**1 teaspoon baking soda**
>**¼ teaspoon salt**

Cream:

>**1 stick salted butter with**
>**1¾ cups brown sugar, well packed**

Beginning and ending with the flour, add alternately to the creamed mixture the sifted ingredients and:

>**3 eggs**
>**½ cup sour cream**
>**chocolate water**

Flavor with:

>**1 teaspoon almond extract**

Pour batter into greased 9-inch square pan. Bake 50 minutes or

until cake tester comes out clean. Cool. Slice lengthwise. Fill with raspberry jam. Frost with:

Almond Fluff Topping, page 73

Decorate with blanched almonds.

Génoise au Chocolat

This batter is used widely in Europe, where its natural egg leavening is preferred to baking powder leavening. It's a bit tricky to make the first time, but the knack is quickly acquired.

Preheat oven to 350°.
Melt:

1 stick sweet butter

Let stand 5 minutes, then carefully pour into a spouted cup, leaving the slight sediment at the bottom of the pan. This is now clarified butter. Reserve.
Over warm water in the top of a large double boiler, beat:

6 eggs

until doubled in bulk, using an electric beater at high speed or a whip for about 15 minutes. Remove from the heat and continue to beat until cold. Sift over the mixture and fold in lightly with a spatula:

⅔ cup all-purpose flour
⅓ cup cocoa

Distribute the flour evenly but do not mix. Then gradually fold in clarified butter in a slow stream. With sweet butter, grease 2 round 9-inch pans and dust lightly with a mixture of flour and cocoa. Divide the batter and pour into greased pans. Bake 40 to 45 minutes or until done. Remove from pan at once. Cool on a rack. Fill with apricot jam and frost with:

Chocolate or Mocha Butter Cream, pages 70-71

Decorate with rosettes.

Pour into 15×10×1-inch pan, lined with greased waxed paper. Bake 30 to 40 minutes. Loosen around the edges and turn out onto a towel sprinkled with confectioners' sugar. Remove the paper; trim off edges of the cake. Roll the cake immediately with the towel. Cool.

Meanwhile, combine:

>   **2 tablespoons honey**
>   **1½ teaspoons warm water**

and bring just to boil over moderate heat, stirring constantly. Remove from heat. Add:

>   **½ cup chocolate pieces**
>   **½ teaspoon vanilla**

Stir until the chocolate pieces melt and the mixture is smooth. Cool about 10 minutes. Fold in:

>   **¾ cup heavy cream, whipped**

Chill until thick enough to spread. Unroll the cake. Spread the cake with the chocolate mixture; roll the cake again. Chill several hours or wrap in foil and freeze.

To serve, sprinkle with sifted confectioners' sugar. Cut into slices. Makes about 12 servings.

Viennese Chocolate Roll

From experience and against all established principles I advise you not to line the baking sheet with waxed paper.

Preheat oven to 400°.

Grease a jelly roll pan. Flour lightly. Sift together 3 times:

>   **¼ cup sifted all-purpose flour**
>   **½ teaspoon salt**
>   **4 tablespoons cocoa**
>   **1 cup sifted confectioners' sugar**

Beat:

>   **5 egg yolks**

until thick. Put on top of them, without mixing:

>   **1 teaspoon grated orange rind**
>   **1 teaspoon vanilla**

Gently fold the dry ingredients into the yolks. Beat with a clean beater:

5 egg whites

until they hold in glossy peaks. Fold into the batter. Spread into the pan. Bake 15 minutes. Have a clean damp kitchen towel ready. Work quickly as soon as it comes out of the oven. Use a sharp knife to separate ½ inch of the cake all around the pan. Loosen the *cake* with a spatula. Leave the edges in the pan. Slide the cake onto the damp cloth. Roll up at once in the towel and store in the refrigerator until ready to use (edges may be used to make Bizochos Borrachos, page 27). One hour before serving, whip:

½ cup heavy cream

Fold in:

½ cup Swiss-type sour cherry jam
1 teaspoon cinnamon

Spread this mixture from left to right on the cake except for the last inch. It will spread properly when rolled.

Bûche de Noël

Bake a roll according to directions for Viennese Chocolate Roll, page 21. Make 2 cups Mocha Butter Cream, page 70, and 1 cup Chocolate Butter Cream, page 71. Spread the roll with Mocha Butter Cream. Roll. Frost top and sides with mocha and chocolate butter creams to create a log with wood and bark. Score with a fork to design the bark. Decorate with green butter cream (use food coloring), marzipan holly leaves, and red butter cream for berries and leaves.

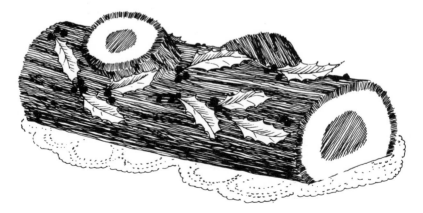

in:

> ½ cup dark rum
> ½ cup cold tea

Make 1 recipe Soft Chocolate Custard, page 136. Cool. You may add chopped candied fruits that have been marinated in rum to the custard. Use the same rum to soak the sponge cake.

Place 1 layer of the cake in the bottom of an ovenproof dish. Pour ½ the custard over it. Repeat. Chill.

Make a meringue by beating:

> **4 egg whites**

until frothy, gradually adding:

> ½ teaspoon vanilla
> ¼ cup granulated sugar

Continue beating until mixture holds a peak.

Top the cake with meringue. Place in a 225° oven until lightly browned. Chill again before serving.

Creole Sponge Cake

Preheat oven to 350°.

Dissolve:

> **4 ounces unsweetened chocolate in**
> **¾ cup milk**
> **¼ cup light rum**

Beat until frothy and pale:

> **4 egg yolks**

Gradually add:

> **2 cups granulated sugar**

Sift:

> **1 cup flour**
> **1 teaspoon baking powder**

Fold with the melted chocolate into the egg mixture.

Fold in:

> **4 stiffly beaten egg whites**

Bake in two 8-inch layer pans 30 to 35 minutes.
Fill and frost with:

Sweet Chocolate Glaze, page 62

Summer Cake

Start 24 hours ahead.
Line a 2-quart-size springform pudding mold with 3 packages of lady fingers.
You will have some leftover. Reserve.
Mix:

¼ cup tea

with:

¼ cup rum

Sprinkle the lady fingers with this mixture.
Beat:

2 pints heavy cream

until its stands in peaks with:

⅓ cup superfine sugar
1 teaspoon vanilla

Incorporate the contents of:

1 jar of Raffeto Italian fruit mélange
½ cup of crushed marrons glaces
¼ cup Dutch process cocoa

Turn into the lined mold.
Use the rest of the lady fingers to cover the cream. Cover with aluminum foil and place into the refrigerator until ready to use. Then unmold with the bottom facing up and garnish with grated chocolate and a ring of whipped cream.

Bizcochos Borrachos

A Spanish pre-siesta snack.

In a glass or crystal bowl over:

> 12 ladyfingers or equivalent amount
> of sponge cake

spoon:

> ½ cup crème de cacao
> ¼ cup light rum

Cover with Rocky Road Sauce, page 131. Chill. Serves 4.

Celso Terra's Orpheo Negro Cake

This cake, created by the late Brazilian poet to celebrate the film, Black Orpheus, *has an unprecedented three-layer richness. To make it, you need three 9-inch buttered and floured layer pans.*

Preheat the oven to 375°.
In the top of a double boiler, combine:

> 1 cup dark brown sugar, well packed
> ½ cup water
> ½ cup milk
> 3 ounces unsweetened chocolate

and cook over hot, but not boiling, water until the chocolate melts. Cool and reserve. In a large bowl, cream together:

> 2 sticks sweet butter
> ¼ teaspoon salt
> 1 cup dark brown sugar, well packed
> 2 teaspoons vanilla

Sift together twice:

> 2 cups all-purpose flour
> 2 teaspoons baking powder
> 3 tablespoons cocoa

Alternately add to the large bowl mixture:

> 10 egg yolks

and the flour mixture, beginning and ending with flour.
Beat well after each addition. Combine with melted chocolate mixture.
Beat the batter an extra half minute, turn into pans, and bake 25 minutes.
Cool 10 minutes in pans, then turn onto wire racks to finish cooling.
Fill and frost with:

> **Fudge Frosting, page 65**

Sprinkle with shaved or chopped Brazil nuts. Garnish top with:

> **10 moist pitted prunes filled with some
> of the frosting**

Old-Fashioned Cocoa Fruit Cake

Preheat oven to 300°.
In a large bowl, cream together:

> **2 sticks salted butter
> 3¼ cups granulated sugar**

Sift together:

> **3 cups all-purpose flour
> ½ cup cocoa
> 2 teaspoons baking powder
> 2 teaspoons baking soda
> ½ teaspoon salt
> ½ teaspoon powdered mace
> ½ teaspoon cinnamon**

Cut with kitchen scissors to the size of raisins, and place in a bowl:

> **2 cups figs
> 1 cup pitted dates**

Reserve.
To the creamed butter and sugar mixture, add alternately:

> **6 eggs**

and the dry ingredients, beating well after each addition.
Then add, still beating:

> **¾ cup bourbon**

To the figs and the dates, add:

> 2 cups black raisins
> 1 cup currants
> 1 teaspoon grated orange rind
> 1 cup chopped almonds
> 2 tablespoons flour

Mix until all the fruit is coated with flour, then blend into the batter.
Pour into a buttered kugelhopf mold and bake for 2 hours, or until a cake tester comes out clean.
If batter is used for two smaller cakes, reduce the baking to 45 to 50 minutes.

Gâteau aux Marrons

Preheat oven to 350°.
Cream:

> 1½ sticks sweet butter
> 1 cup granulated sugar
> 6 tablespoons cocoa

Add, one at a time:

> 5 egg yolks

and continue beating for 30 seconds.
Beat:

> 5 egg whites

into the batter with:

> ½ cup ground blanched almonds
> ¾ cup sweetened chestnut purée

Bake in a well-buttered spring mold for 45 minutes. When cool, slice into three layers with a cake wire. Spread two layers with:

> 1 cup raspberry jam thinned to spreading
>   consistency with
> 2 tablespoons Grand Marnier

Shape the cake with the plain layer on top.
Frost sides with:

> 1 cup chestnut purée

Ice top with:

> Glossy Chocolate Icing, page 61

Before the icing sets, garnish the cake with marrons glacés.

Le Gâteau de ma Tante

Preheat the oven to 375°.
In a saucepan combine:

> 2 teaspoons sweet butter
> ½ cup cold water
> ⅛ teaspoon salt

Bring to a boil. Add all at once:

> ½ cup flour

stirring vigorously until the mixture forms a ball. Remove from the heat.
Beat in one at a time:

> 2 eggs

and continue until the mixture is smooth. Grease and lightly flour a baking
sheet. Using a pastry tube filled with the mixture, trace a circle on the sheet
and fill it with the rest of the paste. Brush with:

> 1 beaten egg

Sprinkle top with:

> ½ cup slivered almonds

Bake for 30 minutes until well risen and browned. Cool completely.
Melt:

> 4 ounces sweet chocolate with 3 tablespoons of coffee

Moisten:

> 1 tablespoon gelatin

with a little cold water and:

> 1 tablespoon dark rum

Beat:

> 1 egg + egg yolk

with:

> 3 tablespoons flour
> 3 tablespoons granulated sugar

until very smooth.
Add the chocolate and the gelatin.
Heat:

> ¾ cup half and half

pour in the mixture and bring to a boil, stirring all the while. Then instantly remove the custard from the heat continuing to stir. If it is not thick enough to coat the spoon, return it to the heat. Cool, then place in the refrigerator until it just begins to set.
Meanwhile, beat:

> 1 egg white

until stiff and incorporate it in the cream. Chill again and allow to set.
Beat:

> 1½ cups heavy cream

until it stands in glossy peaks and add:

> ½ cup of praline powder, (page 194)

Split the cooled cake into halves.
Fill the bottom with the rum cream and the top with the whipped cream mixture. Reassemble the halves. Dust the top with grated sweet chocolate.

Cocoa Cinnamon Pound Cake

Preheat oven to 325°.
Cream until light and fluffy:

> 1 cup salted butter or margarine

Add gradually:

> 2½ cups sugar

Add, one at a time, beating well after each addition:

> 5 eggs

Sift together on a sheet of waxed paper:

> **3 cups sifted all-purpose flour**
> **½ teaspoon salt**
> **½ teaspoon baking powder**
> **½ cup cocoa**
> **1 teaspoon cinnamon**

Mix the dry ingredients into the creamed mixture alternately with:

> **1 cup milk**

Beat 3 seconds.
Add:

> **1 teaspoon vanilla**

Pour the batter into a greased and floured 10-inch tube pan, or a 3-quart kugelhopf pan.
Bake for 1½ hours or until done. Cool for 15 minutes, then remove from pan.
Serve unfrosted or with:

> **Cherry or Honey or Orange Topping,**
>   **pages 72, 73, 74**

Upside-Down Aztec Sunburst Cake

This cake takes a little time to put together but it comes out of the pan already beautifully decorated.

Preheat oven to 350°.
Melt in a 9-inch square pan:

> **¼ cup sweet butter or margarine**

Add:

> **½ cup brown sugar, well packed**
> **2 tablespoons light corn syrup**

Mix well. Spread evenly over the bottom of the pan.
Take:

> **4 canned pear halves**

from a 16-ounce can. Drain well, then slice each pear into four sections and place in a sunburst design over the mixture in the pan. Between the pear sections, arrange:

> ¼ cup quartered maraschino cherries
> ¼ cup chopped pecans

To make the batter, sift together on waxed paper:

> 1½ cups sifted all-purpose flour
> ¼ cup cocoa
> ½ teaspoon baking soda
> ½ teaspoon salt

In a large mixing bowl cream together:

> ½ cup plus 2 tablespoons sweet butter or
>   margarine
> 1¼ cups sugar
> 1 teaspoon vanilla

Add, one at a time, beating well after each addition:

> 2 eggs

To the creamed mixture add the sifted dry ingredients alternately with:

> ½ cup buttermilk

Beat well. Pour the batter over fruit and nuts in pan.
Bake for 45 to 55 minutes or until done. Immediately invert pan on serving plate. Serve warm, with whipped cream. Makes 9 to 12 servings.

Haitian Upside-Down Cake

Preheat oven to 350°.
Cream together:

> 4 tablespoons salted butter
> ¼ cup dark brown sugar, well packed

Mix in:

> ¾ cup light corn syrup
> 1 cup chopped peanuts

Grease a 9×12-inch pan and spread mixture on the bottom of the pan. Cream together:

> **6 tablespoons salted butter**
> **1¼ cups sugar**

until light.
Meanwhile, melt:

> **4 ounces unsweetened chocolate**

over hot, but not boiling, water.
Beat into the butter and sugar mixture:

> **2 egg yolks**

and add:

> **melted chocolate**
> **1 teaspoon vanilla**

Sift:

> **2 cups flour**

with:

> **2 tablespoons baking powder**

Add the dry ingredients to the chocolate mixture alternately with:

> **1½ cups milk**

Beat until stiff and fold into the batter:

> **2 egg whites**

Pour into the cake pan and bake 55 minutes. Invert on a board or platter, cool, and serve cut in squares.

Apricot or Tangerine Upside-Down Chocolate Cake

Melt:

> **½ cup firmly packed brown sugar with**
> **¼ cup salted butter**

Spread in a greased 9-inch square pan. Drain:

> 1 pound canned apricot halves or
> tangerine sections

Reserve the syrup. Arrange the fruit on the sugar mixture (apricots' rounded sides up). Sprinkle with:

> 2 tablespoons of the syrup
> ⅔ cup dried coconut flakes

Preheat oven to 350°. Then make the cake batter. In a saucepan over hot, but not boiling, water, melt:

> 4 ounces sweet chocolate

Sift:

> 1½ cups sifted cake flour
> 1 cup granulated sugar
> ½ teaspoon baking soda
> ½ teaspoon baking powder
> ½ teaspoon salt

Place:

> 6 tablespoons softened sweet butter

in a large mixing bowl. Add dry ingredients. Measure:

> ¾ cup buttermilk

and add half of it to the flour mixture. Mix until all the flour is dampened. Beat 2 minutes at medium speed or 300 strokes by hand.
Add:

> the chocolate
> 2 eggs
> remaining buttermilk
> 1 teaspoon vanilla

Beat 1 minute longer, or 150 strokes.
Pour over the fruit. Bake 45 to 50 minutes. Cool in pan 5 minutes, then invert on a serving platter. Let stand 1 minute before removing the pan. Serve warm with:

> Chocolate Cinnamon-Flecked Topping,
> page 74

Chocolate Applesauce Cake

Preheat oven to 350°.
Sift together in a large bowl:

> 2½ cups cake flour
> ⅓ cup cocoa
> 2 teaspoons baking soda
> ¼ teaspoon salt
> 1 teaspoon mace
> ½ teaspoon ginger
> ½ teaspoon cloves
> ½ teaspoon allspice

Add:

> 1 teaspoon grated lime peel

Combine in a second bowl:

> 2 cups chopped walnuts
> 2 cups seedless raisins
> 1 cup chopped dates
> ½ cup chopped dried apricots

and dust one-half of the dry mixture over the fruits.
Cream:

> 1 stick salted butter
> ¾ cup brown sugar
> 2 cups applesauce

Add the rest of the dry mixture in small amounts, beating well after each addition. Carefully fold in the floured fruits. Bake 1 hour in a 10×15-inch greased loaf pan.

Buttermilk Mocha Cake

A lovely moist three-layer cake.

Preheat oven to 350°.
Sift together:

> 2¾ cups cake flour
> ¼ teaspoon salt
> 1½ teaspoons baking soda

Reserve.
Over very low heat, melt:

4½ ounces semisweet chocolate in
¾ cup hot water

Stir to blend, then remove from heat and reserve. In the large bowl of the electric mixer, cream:

1½ sticks softened sweet butter
1 cup granulated sugar
1 teaspoon vanilla

Add:

3 eggs

Beat at high speed until fluffy, about 5 minutes. Blend in the melted chocolate, then add alternately the sifted dry ingredients and:

1 cup buttermilk

Bake in 3 greased 9-inch layer pans for 20 to 25 minutes. Test after 20 minutes and watch carefully so as not to overbake. This is essential to retain moisture. Frost with:

Mocha Cocoa Frosting, page 68

Florida Shortcake

Preheat oven to 350°.
In a large mixing bowl, sift together:

1⅔ cups sifted flour
4 teaspoons baking powder
⅓ cup cocoa
½ teaspoon salt
¼ cup granulated sugar

Cut in:

4 tablespoons sweet butter

Beat into a measuring cup:

1 egg

and fill it to the one-half cup mark with:

milk

Add this mixture to the dry ingredients, stirring rapidly until a soft dough is formed, adding extra milk by the teaspoonful if necessary to ease the texture, which should not become sticky. Knead for a few seconds on a floured pastry board. Divide in half and pat the dough into two 8-inch layer pans. Bake 12 minutes. Divide:

> 6 seedless oranges

in sections. Remove membrane. Place sections between layers and on top of cake on rimmed serving platter. Combine:

> 1 cup orange juice
> 1 cup granulated sugar
> 1 tablespoon grated orange peel
> 1 tablespoon brandy

Bring to a boil, stirring to melt the sugar. Pour over the shortcake. Serve with:

> Chocolate-Flecked Whipped Cream,
> page 132

Adele's Icebox Cake

French Petits Beurres can stand longer dipping because they are harder than Social Teas, which may become so soft that it is difficult to spread the cream on them.

Cream together until white and fluffy:

> 1 pound sifted confectioners' sugar
> 1 pound sweet butter

Dip, one at a time, 48 Petits Beurres or Social Tea Biscuits in a cup of cold double-strength coffee.

Arrange on a cookie sheet to form a rectangle of 8 cookies. Spread with creamed mixture, then sift a dusting from:

> ¾ cup chocolate instant drink mix

over the layer. Repeat 6 times.

Frost the sides and dust with remaining cocoa.

Garnish the top with chocolate curls, page 8, candied violets and rose petals, page 200, and silver nonpareils. Make it gaudy. This is a very Victorian cake.

Blended Chocolate Cheesecake

Prepare a gingersnap crust as for Brandy Black-Bottom Pie, page 114.
In the blender put:

> 1 tablespoon unflavored gelatin
> 1 tablespoon frozen orange juice
> ½ cup hot water

Cover and blend 40 seconds. Add:

> ½ cup superfine granulated sugar
> 2 egg yolks
> 8 ounces cream cheese

Cover and blend 10 seconds. Add:

> 1 cup crushed ice
> 1 cup sour cream

Cover. Blend 15 seconds. In a saucepan over hot, but not boiling, water, melt:

> 4 ounces sweet chocolate

Fold into the cheese mixture. Pour into the pie crust. Chill. Decorate with chocolate curls.

VARIATION:

Use ½ the gingersnap crust recipe. Pat it on the bottom of the springform (10-inch) pan. Follow above directions.
Serve with:

> **Cherry Topping, page 74**

Chocolate Ricotta Cassata

An elegant Italian cheesecake. Ricotta is made from whey with whole milk added. Moist ricotta resembles cottage cheese curd in consistency.

Cut:

> 1 pound cake (9×5 inches)

horizontally into 4 slices about ½ inch thick. Press:

>1 pound fresh ricotta cheese

through a coarse sieve into a bowl. Add:

>2 tablespoons heavy cream
>¼ cup granulated sugar
>3 tablespoons triple sec or Curaçao

Beat until smooth. Fold in:

>1 tablespoon coarsely chopped red candied
>   cherries
>1 tablespoon green candied cherries
>1 tablespoon candied pineapple
>⅓ cup semisweet chocolate pieces,
>   finely chopped

Place the bottom slice of cake on a serving plate. Spread the cheese filling generously between the 4 layers of the cake. Gently press the loaf together. Chill about 2 hours (filling appears soft but becomes firm when chilled). Frost with:

>### Rich Chocolate Frosting, page 68

Spread frosting evenly over top and sides of the cassata. To decorate, pipe remaining frosting through decorator tube. Cover loosely and keep in refrigerator 24 hours before serving.

Fudge Date Cake

Preheat oven to 325°.
In a saucepan over hot, but not boiling, water, melt:

>4 ounces unsweetened chocolate
>1 cup granulated sugar

stirring until smooth. Add:

>1 cup milk

Beat until light:

>4 egg yolks
>1 cup granulated sugar

Fold the yolk mixture into the chocolate. Sift together on waxed paper and pour into a large bowl:

> 1¼ cups sifted cake flour
> 3 teaspoons baking powder
> ¼ teaspoon salt

Gradually mix the sifted ingredients into the chocolate mixture. In a separate bowl, place:

> ¾ cup chopped pitted dates
> ½ cup chopped walnuts
> 2 tablespoons grated orange rind
> 1 teaspoon vanilla
> ⅛ teaspoon mace
> 2 tablespoons all-purpose flour

Mix well so that all the fruit is dusted with flour. Fold into batter.
Beat until they hold glossy peaks:

> **4 egg whites**

Gently fold into the batter.
Pour into a greased 9-inch tube pan. Bake for 40 minutes or until cake tester comes out clean. Garnish with:

> **Royal Icing, page 63**

Decorate with walnut halves and glacé cherries.

Upside-Down Cake Squares

Preheat oven to 375°.
In a saucepan over hot, not boiling, water, melt:

> **1 cup semisweet chocolate pieces**

Add:

> **⅔ cup sweetened condensed milk**
> **1 teaspoon vanilla**
> **½ cup chopped nuts**

Stir until blended. Pour into a 13×9×2-inch baking pan lined with waxed paper.
Prepare your favorite:

> **white or yellow cake mix**

Pour gently over chocolate mixture to cover it. Bake 45 minutes. Invert cake on rack and remove pan. Let stand 10 minutes. Remove waxed paper, then turn on wire racks to finish cooling. Cut into 2 dozen 2-inch squares.

Cocoa Cupcakes

Preheat oven to 375°.
Sift together four times:

> 3 cups all-purpose flour
> ½ cup cocoa
> 1 teaspoon salt
> 1 teaspoon cinnamon
> 3 teaspoons baking soda

Cream until fluffy:

> 2 sticks salted butter
> 1½ cups brown sugar, well packed

Beat into the butter mixture:

> 3 egg yolks
> 1 teaspoon vanilla

Add the sifted dry ingredients and:

> 2 cups sour cream

alternately in small amounts and beat carefully after each addition. Bake 20 to 25 minutes. Frost as desired. Makes 36 cupcakes.

Chocolate Syrup Cupcakes

Preheat oven to 375°.
Cream together until light and fluffy:

> ½ cup sweet butter or margarine
> 1 cup sugar
> 1 teaspoon vanilla

Add, one at a time, beating well after each addition:

> **4 eggs**

Combine:

> **1¼ cups all-purpose flour**
> **¾ teaspoon baking soda**

and add alternately to creamed mixture with:

> **1½ cups Cocoa Syrup, page 130**

Pour batter into paper-lined muffin tins, filling each one-half full. Bake for 20 to 25 minutes. Frost with:

> **Fudge Frosting, page 65**

Makes 30 cupcakes.

Chocolate Yeast Cake

Prepare one day ahead.

In a large bowl, cream together:

> **2 sticks softened sweet butter**
> **2½ cups granulated sugar**
> **3 eggs**

Dilute:

> **½ yeast cake or envelope in**
> **½ cup lukewarm water**

Add to butter and egg mixture. Sift together:

> **½ cup cocoa**
> **1 teaspoon almond extract**
> **3 cups flour**
> **1 teaspoon baking soda**
> **⅛ teaspoon salt**

Add the dry ingredients alternately with:

> **2½ cups milk**

to the mixture in the large bowl, beating well after each addition. Add:

> **1 cup finely chopped and floured almonds**
> **12 chopped and floured glacé cherries**

Pour in a buttered kugelhopf mold and refrigerate overnight.
Preheat oven to 300°. Bake for 45 minutes. Unmold on a cake rack. Dust
with a mixture of:

> 1 teaspoon cinnamon
> ¼ cup sifted confectioners' sugar

Chocolate Custard Coffee Cake

Preheat oven to 350°.
Sift together:

> 3 cups all-purpose flour
> 6 tablespoons granulated sugar
> 1 tablespoon baking powder
> 1½ teaspoons salt

Cut in:

> 1 stick salted butter

until mixture resembles coarse crumbs. Beat together:

> 2 whole eggs
> 1 egg yolk

Stir in to blend:

> ½ cup milk

Add liquid all at once to flour mixture, stirring until flour is well moistened.
If necessary, add more milk to make a soft dough. Turn onto a lightly floured
surface, knead gently 30 seconds. Roll the dough into a 10×20-inch
rectangle. Spread:

> 1 cup Soft Chocolate Custard, **page 136**

over center third of the dough. Roll up and seal the seam. Place seam
down on a greased baking sheet; shape into a ring. Pinch edges together.
Slash with scissors at 3-inch intervals, not cutting completely through to
center of the ring. The custard will show through the slash. Beat:

> 1 egg white

until frothy and brush over the top. Sprinkle with:

> 2 tablespoons granulated sugar

Bake 20 to 25 minutes, or until done.

Torten

Torten differ from cakes only in that the flour is replaced with ground nuts or sweet crumbs. Nuts add a rich flavor and a special texture. Torten are leavened by large quantities of beaten eggs. They are delicious and not difficult to make. Yolks must be beaten to a real froth, for they have to hold heavy nuts in suspension. The egg whites must not be overbeaten; they should expand with the heat. Use a whisk for torten. The result is worth the added effort. Fold delicately.

Some famous regional specialties are really cakes baked to look like torten. These have been included here.

Almond Torte Squares

A modest looking dessert, this is a superlative, light-as-a-feather, brownie-type cookie. It does not store well because of its high egg yolk content and must be eaten right away. It is beautiful enough for a finale to a formal

45

luncheon, served with coffee. A sandwich of these squares, filled with almond flavored whipped cream, page 132, would also be interesting.

Preheat oven to 325°.

In a saucepan over hot, but not boiling, water, soften:

> **1 stick sweet butter**
> **2 ounces semisweet chocolate**

Meanwhile, grind enough almonds to make:

> **1 cup**

Make:

> **2 tablespoons cracker meal from unflavored**
> **cracker crumbs**

Beat together:

> **3 egg yolks**
> **1 cup confectioners' sugar**

until light and frothy. Fold in the almond and cracker meal. Blend the melted chocolate and butter mixture until smooth, and then fold into the almond mixture. Flavor with:

> **1 teaspoon vanilla**
> **1 teaspoon almond extract**

Beat until they stand in peaks:

> **4 egg whites**

Fold into the batter.

Pour into a buttered 9×10-inch or 8×12-inch pan. Sprinkle with:

> **½ cup shaved almonds**

for decoration.

Bake 30 to 35 minutes. Cool before cutting into 4-inch squares. Dribble almond Royal Icing, page 63, over the top.

Chocolate Revanie

A classic Syrian cake to which an American added a chocolate touch, this cake is made from leftover chocolate cake.

Remove all filling and frosting from the leftover cake. Coarsely break it

into crumbs, place it on a cookie sheet and dry in the oven at 200°. Cool.
Roll into fine crumbs, enough to make 1 cup.

Preheat oven to 350°.

In a mixing bowl, combine:

> **the chocolate cake crumbs**
> **1½ cups finely ground walnuts**
> **grated rind of 1 orange**

In another mixing bowl, beat until they are stiff:

> **6 egg whites**

In still another bowl, beat:

> **6 egg yolks**
> **¾ cup granulated sugar**
> **1 teaspoon vanilla**

until mixture is light and lemon-colored.

Gradually fold the beaten egg whites into the yolk mixture. Then fold in the nut mixture. Pour the batter into a greased baking pan, 13×9½×2-inch. Bake for 45 minutes.

Meanwhile, prepare a syrup as follows. In a saucepan combine:

> **¾ cup sugar**
> **2¼ cups water**
> **½ of a cinnamon stick**
> **1 orange slice**

Bring to a boil over low heat and simmer until the sugar is completely dissolved.

When the cake is ready to be removed from the oven, add to the syrup:

> **½ cup crème de cacao**

Remove the cake from the oven and immediately pour the hot syrup over it. Cool the cake in the pan. Cut the cake into diamond shapes for serving. This recipe yields about 24 pieces.

Spanish Mocha Torte

Split 2 layers of sponge cake to make 4. Reserve. Whip:

> **2 cups heavy cream**

until thick. Then sift together and gradually add:

> 3 tablespoons cocoa
> 2 tablespoons powdered instant coffee
> 2 tablespoons confectioners' sugar

beating until the cream holds a peak.
Make:

> 2 cups Fudge Sauce, **page 128**

Moisten the layers with:

> ½ cup crème de cacao

diluted with:

> ¼ cup tea

Spread 2 layers with Chocolate Fudge Sauce, page 128, and 2 layers with cocoa whipped cream. Frost sides with remaining whipped cream. Chill. Garnish with glacé cherries just before serving.

Sacher Torte

Madame Sacher's famous Viennese recipe for the home baker. The chocolate is the thing. You must use French, Swiss, or Dutch dark Caraque chocolate or bittersweet pastilles.

Preheat oven to 300°.
Soften:

> 3½ ounces chocolate

on aluminum foil over the pilot light.
Cream:

> 1⅝ sticks sweet butter

with chocolate. Add:

> ¾ cup superfine granulated sugar

Beat:

> 5 egg yolks

one at a time into the mixture, alternating with:

> ¼ cup cake flour

Beat with another beater in a large bowl:

> 5 egg whites
> ¾ cup superfine granulated sugar

until egg whites hold glossy peaks. Fold the batter into the whites very gently.
Butter a decorative quart-size cake mold. Flour it lightly with:

> 1 tablespoon mixture of confectioners'
> sugar, cocoa, and flour

Turn the batter into it.
Bake 45 minutes or until cake tester comes out clean.
Turn the mold over onto a rack. After 5 minutes, tape it to remove the cake.
It drops. Cool 10 minutes. Spread with:

> 1 cup warm apricot jam

Working very quickly, cover the jam with:

> **Chocolate Icing, page 61**

Cool for several hours before serving, but do not refrigerate or the icing
will show beads of moisture.

Hungarian Dobosch Torte

You need seven 8-inch layer pans.

Preheat oven to 350°.
Beat until thick and lemon-colored:

> 7 egg yolks

Gradually add:

> 1 cup confectioners' sugar

Sift three times:

> 1 cup sifted cake flour

with:

> ¼ teaspoon salt

Fold into yolk mixture. Beat to hold a soft peak:

> 7 egg whites

Fold in.

Line layer pans with waxed paper, then butter the paper with softened butter. *Divide the batter among the seven pans.* Bake 12 minutes in 2 batches. Don't crowd the oven. Remove at once from the pans. Cool. Peel off the paper.
Fill between layers with:

Hard Chocolate Icing, page 61

Then ice the top and sides. Stick a few toothpicks through the top layers to keep them in place. Remove them before serving.

Cocoa Peach Torte

Preheat oven to 350°. Grease bottom of a 9×1½-inch springform pan. Combine:

> 1⅓ cups all-purpose flour
> 1 teaspoon baking powder
> ⅓ cup sugar

Cut in:

> ½ cup softened sweet butter or margarine

until mixture is crumbly. Add:

> 1 egg, slightly beaten

and blend until flour is moistened. Pat the dough evenly on the bottom and up the sides of springform pan 2 inches high.

FILLING:

Cream in small mixer bowl:

> ½ cup sweet butter
> ¼ cup cocoa
> 6 tablespoons sugar

Add, one at a time, beating well after each addition:

> 2 eggs

Blend in:

> ½ teaspoon almond extract
> 1 cup ground almonds

Pour filling into shell. Bake 40 to 45 minutes or until the shell is lightly browned. Cool. Spring the edge of the mold. Top with:

> 2 cups cooked sliced peaches, drained

Arrange on top of torte. Chill, then glaze with:

> ⅓ cup peach preserves

mixed with:

> ¼ teaspoon lemon juice

Pipe the rim with:

> 1 cup whipped sweetened cream

Makes 10 servings.

Linzer Torte

A slight variation of the classic recipe, but still found in some Viennese pastry shops.

Preheat oven to 350°.
In a large mixing bowl, work together with the hands until the dough feels like clay:

> 1½ sticks sweet butter
> 1 cup granulated sugar
> 1 sieved hard-cooked egg yolk
> 2 eggs
> 1 cup unblanched ground almonds
> ½ teaspoon cinnamon
> ¼ teaspoon cloves
> 1 tablespoon grated orange peel
> 1 tablespoon cocoa
> ¼ teaspoon salt
> 1¼ cups sifted all-purpose flour

Spread the dough ¼ inch thick in a 10-inch springform. To form a pie shell, build up sides one inch high. Brush the bottom lightly with raspberry jam. Place the remaining dough in a pastry bag and pipe an edge and a lattice over the shell. Bake 30 to 35 minutes.

Before serving, fill the hollows in the lattice with about:

> 1½ cups raspberry jam

flavored with:

> 2 teaspoons brandy, rum, or cognac

Panforte di Siena

A nutty torte.

Preheat oven to 300°.
In a bowl, combine:

> ¼ pound blanched almonds
> ¼ pound toasted hazelnuts
> ½ cup cocoa
> 2 teaspoons cinnamon
> ½ teaspoon grated orange rind
> ½ cup flour
> 1 cup finely shredded candied orange peel
> ½ cup candied cherries

In a large saucepan, combine:

> ¾ cup honey
> ¾ cup granulated sugar
> ¾ cup water

Bring to a boil over medium heat, stirring constantly until the mixture reaches the soft ball stage (238° on the candy thermometer). Add to the fruit and nut mixture and mix well. Turn into a 9-inch springform pan lined with buttered paper and bake 30 minutes.

Put the pan, bottom up, on top of a cup to cool and spring the sides from the bottom. When cool slide it to a serving platter. Sprinkle with:

> 2 tablespoons confectioners' sugar

mixed with:

> 1 tablespoon cinnamon

and serve.

Meringues

A meringue is baked slowly to dry out the batter. A 175° warming oven is best. Meringues may be left 6 to 8 hours and will come out as lightly colored as those in the bake shops. Meringues may be baked in a 225° oven for two hours.

If you like chewy meringues, raise the temperature to 275°. Bake only 1½ hours whatever the size of the meringue.

Four egg whites (grade A) beaten with ½ pound sugar will yield enough meringue for 12 3-inch diameter shells or a 9-inch pie shell or an 8-inch Schaumtorte.

For meringue, a rotary or an electric beater is as good as a whisk and much faster.

Leftover egg whites frozen in ice trays that are covered with plastic bags may be baked on a bright, sunny day—best for meringue baking as they tend to become sticky in moist air. Fresh or stored egg whites should be brought to a temperature of 70° for best whipping.

Cocoa Meringues

Fold:

> ½ cup sweet chocolate pieces

into:

> 4-egg-white meringue batter

The pieces will be suspended in the batter. While baking, the chocolate will melt and make dark brown, somewhat chewy spots in the meringue. Cocoa Meringues may be substituted for any regular meringue recipe.

Cocoa Schaumtorte

Preheat the oven to 225°.
Beat until they are foamy:

> 6 egg whites with
> ⅛ teaspoon salt

Continue to beat, adding gradually:

> 1 teaspoon almond extract
> 2 cups sifted confectioners' sugar
> ⅓ cup sifted cocoa

until the eggs hold a glossy peak.
Pour ⅔ of this mixture in an oiled 10-inch springform, spreading some of the batter to the top of the sides. Drop the rest from a teaspoon on an oiled baking sheet to form small kisses. Bake 2 hours.
Turn off and open the oven. Leave the meringues until cold.
Spring the sides of the mold.
Gently slide the meringue shell on a serving platter. Fill with whipped cream and berries or with ice cream. Quickly stick the kisses half on the edge of the meringue, half on the edge of the mounded filling to decorate.

French Dacquoise

Preheat oven to 250°.
Beat in a large mixing bowl until frothy:

> **5 egg whites**

with:

> **⅛ teaspoon cream of tartar**

Gradually add:

> **¾ cup granulated sugar**

while beating. Continue beating until the meringue stands in stiff peaks when the beater is raised from the mixing bowl.
In another bowl, blend:

> **½ cup granulated sugar**
> **1 cup ground blanched almonds**
> **½ cup zwieback crumbs**
> **2 tablespoons all-purpose flour**
> **2 tablespoons cornstarch**
> **½ teaspoon vanilla**

Fold into the meringue. Grease and flour a baking sheet and place two 8-inch circles of brown or waxed paper on it. Spoon the mixture into a pastry bag fitted with a plain tube with a one-half inch opening. Pipe the mixture out spirally from the center to cover the circles. Bake 45 minutes. Cool. Peel the paper from meringue. Spread each layer of meringue with Chocolate Butter Cream, page 71, and stack. Sprinkle top with confectioners' sugar and shaved chocolate.

Mardi Gras Torte

Preheat oven to 300°.
To make meringue circles, cut four 8-inch circles of brown or waxed paper.
Beat:

> 3 egg whites
> ½ teaspoon almond extract
> ¼ teaspoon salt

until mixed and foamy.
Gradually beat in:

> ¾ cup brown sugar, well packed

Beat until stiff and glossy.
Fold in:

> ½ cup chopped nuts

Spread on the paper circles.
Slide the paper circles onto ungreased cookie sheets.
Sprinkle the top of one circle with:

> 1 teaspoon colored sugar or multicolored
> nonpareils

Bake 35 minutes.

FILLING:

Melt over hot, but not boiling, water:

> 1 cup semisweet chocolate pieces

Cool about 10 minutes.
Beat until creamy:

> 8 ounces cream cheese

Blend in:

> 1 tablespoon milk

Gradually beat in:

> ¾ cup firmly packed brown sugar
> 1 teaspoon vanilla
> ⅛ teaspoon salt

Add cream cheese mixture to cooled, melted chocolate and blend.
Fold in:

> 1 cup whipped cream

Spread three-quarters of the filling on the 3 plain meringue circles. Stack and top with the sugared circle. Cover the sides with the remaining filling. Chill overnight.
Makes 12 wedges.

Chocolate Pavlova

This recipe is a take off from a classic New Zealand type of meringue dessert which contains no chocolate. My friend Dorothy Rosser from Auckland and I decided to try it this way and found it even more delicious. Egg whites should be at room temperature.

Beat:

> 3 egg whites

with:

> ⅛ teaspoon salt

Gradually incorporate:

> 1 cup superfine sugar
> 1 teaspoon vinegar
> 1 teaspoon vanilla
> 1 teaspoon Dutch process cocoa

Continue beating for 10 minutes.

Butter a cookie sheet lightly and dust it with:

> 1 teaspoon cornstarch

shaking off the excess.

Preheat oven to 350°.

With the mixture trace an 8-inch diameter circle on the cookie sheet. Inside the circle pile it high to look like an inverted bowl. Bake 10 minutes. Lower the heat to 250°. Continue baking 45 minutes more. Remove from the oven. The meringue will have cracked in many places, showing a mocha colored crust outside and a light chocolate inside, which will be soft. Expect a fallen center and in it place 1½ cups vanilla-flavored whipped cream.

Garnish with:

> 1 small can very well drained mandarin orange sections
> 2 fresh Kiwi fruit, peeled and sliced
> chocolate curls (optional)

Frostings, Icings, Toppings, and Fillings

I have listed below each cake recipe the most appropriate frostings. Some classical cakes have their own frostings.

Generally, *icing* means a smooth frosting. Sometimes called a *glaze,* it should be stroked on with a spatula dipped in warm water to give a glossy finish before decorating.

Frostings which are unglazed should be applied generously, at least ¼ inch thick, and should cover the top and the sides. Frostings and icings may be decorated with nuts or pastry tube decorations, with sprinkles, non-pareils, candied flowers and fruits, marzipan leaves or chocolate leaves, hearts or initials such as you will find in the candy section of this book. When using a tube pan decorate the edge of the pan tube as well. Use taste and restraint. Stay away from that too professional look; keep the decoration naïve. A homemade cake should never look like one that comes from a pastry shop. This guarantees that your effort will be appreciated.

Toppings are creamy, fruity, or nutty mixtures which do *not* cover the sides of the cakes.

Fillings are often, but not always, the same as the frosting. It depends on the recipe. Avoid freezing filled cakes. They do not thaw well.

Cakes must be cooled for boiled icings. Chocolate frostings and fillings are excellent on spice cakes and yellow cakes. Orange icings combine beautifully with chocolate cakes.

> ¾ cup icing will cover a 9-inch round layer
> or 9-inch square.
> 2⅔ cups will fill and frost a three-layer
> 9-inch cake.
> 2½ cups will cover a loaf cake
> 16×5×4 inches.
> 2 cups will fill a 10×15-inch roll.
> 1½ cups will frost 16 to 24 cupcakes,
> depending on size.

Chocolate Italian Meringue, or Boiled Frosting

All boiled frostings have a caramel syrup base. Have all your equipment and ingredients close at hand. You have to work quickly.

Beat:

> **2 egg whites**

only just frothy with:

> **⅛ teaspoon salt**

As the froth begins, slowly pour:

> **½ cup instant chocolate mix**

into them. Reserve for more beating.
To make the caramel syrup, dissolve, stirring in a saucepan with a spout:

> **1 cup granulated sugar**
> **½ cup water**

Over high heat, covered, boil for 2 minutes without stirring. Remove the cover and watch until the syrup reaches the firm ball stage, 244° *on a candy thermometer.* Add this syrup in a ¼-inch stream to the egg white mixture, beating constantly with electric beater at top speed.
When thickening starts, in about 5 minutes, add:

> **1 teaspoon almond extract**

Change from beater to spoon. Continue beating until the frosting is of spreading consistency. Makes 2 cups. Good on Devil's Food Cake, page 13.

Chocolate Coating Used on Top of Italian Meringue Frostings

Double trouble but double pleasure.

In a saucepan over hot, but not boiling, water, melt:

4 ounces semisweet chocolate
½ teaspoon paraffin

Cool and spread this very thin coating with a metal spatula evenly over cold, set frosting. Let it drop down the sides of the cake. Beautiful with Devil's Food Cake, page 13.

Chocolate Marshmallow Boiled Icing

Have all your equipment and ingredients close at hand. Work quickly.

Beat:

2 egg whites

until just frothy, with:

⅛ teaspoon salt

Reserve for more beating.
Make a caramel syrup by dissolving and stirring in a saucepan with a spout:

1½ cups granulated sugar
1⅓ cups water

over high heat. Cover; boil for 2 minutes without stirring. Uncover and watch until the syrup reaches 240° *on a candy thermometer.* Remove from the heat and add:

2 ounces grated semisweet chocolate
24 miniature marshmallows

Let stand until all the bubbles have disappeared.

Add:

> ⅛ teaspoon cream of tartar

Then pour the syrup mixture into the egg whites in a thin stream, beating continually until the icing is of spreading consistency. Ice Devil's Food, Double Chocolate, or any chocolate cake with it. Makes enough for a 3-layer cake. Use a filling of your choice.

Glossy Chocolate Icing

Boil until it spins a thread or reaches 230° on the candy thermometer:

> 1 cup granulated sugar
> ½ cup water

Stir in until melted:

> 4 ounces grated unsweetened chocolate

When the icing coats a spoon, blend in:

> 4 teaspoons peanut oil

Cool. Spread over the cake. Makes 1½ cups, enough for a 3-layer cake. Use filling of your choice.

Hard Chocolate Icing

In a saucepan combine:

> 2 ounces sweet chocolate
> ½ cup granulated sugar
> 4 tablespoons water
> 1 teaspoon vanilla

Cook over medium heat, stirring rapidly with a slotted spoon, rubbing the chocolate against the edges of the pan. When melted, remove from heat and stir until a film forms. Work fast. With a knife dipped in hot water, spread thinly over Dobosch Torte. Makes less than 1 cup.

Sweet Chocolate Glaze

For people with a very sweet tooth.

Melt:

> 4 ounces sweet chocolate

with:

> 1 tablespoon butter
> 4 tablespoons water

Combine in a bowl:

> 1 cup sifted confectioners' sugar
> ⅛ teaspoon salt

Stir in the melted chocolate and:

> 1 teaspoon vanilla

Makes 1 cup.

Icing for Chocolate Éclairs

In a medium-size bowl, place:

> 2 ounces semisweet chocolate

Pour over it:

> 1 cup boiling water

Cover the bowl for 2 minutes. Pour off the water, leaving the melted chocolate. Over it sift:

> 2 cups confectioners' sugar

Add:

> 4 tablespoons heavy cream

and stir to make a spreadable paste. Place the paste over hot water to keep the consistency. Brush the tops of the éclairs in one steady stroke. For 12 éclairs.

Royal Icing

Sift:

> ½ pound confectioners' sugar

Gradually stir in with a whisk:

> 1 tablespoon lemon juice
> 1 egg white, unbeaten

Work together well with a slotted spoon, then spread quickly and allow to dry. Makes 1 cup.

Satiny Glaze

In a saucepan over hot, but not boiling, water, heat:

> ¾ cup semisweet chocolate pieces
> 3 tablespoons salted butter
> 1 tablespoon light corn syrup

Stir constantly until chocolate pieces are melted and mixture is smooth. Add:

> ¼ teaspoon vanilla

Spread warm glaze over top of cake, allowing some to drip down the sides. Makes 1 cup.

Viennese Chocolate Icing

Melt over low heat:

> 4 ounces unsweetened chocolate
> 3 tablespoons frozen orange juice
>   concentrate

Add and blend completely:

> 1 cup confectioners' sugar

Add:

> **2 eggs**
> **6 tablespoons sweet butter**

Beat well. Makes 1 cup.

Cream Cheese Chocolate Frosting

In a saucepan over hot, but not boiling, water, melt:

> **1 ounce semisweet chocolate**

Cream together:

> **3 ounces cream cheese, softened**
> **1 cup confectioners' sugar**

Add:

> **melted chocolate**

and mix. Makes 1 cup.

Cocoa Cream Cheese Frosting

Mix together until well blended:

> **9 ounces softened cream cheese**
> **⅓ cup salted butter**

Sift together:

> **6 cups sifted confectioners' sugar**
> **1 cup cocoa**

Add sugar and cocoa mixture gradually to cheese mixture.
Stir in:

> **5 to 7 tablespoons light cream**

Frosts tops and sides of three 9-inch layers. One-half of recipe makes enough frosting for top of 13×9×2¼-inch sheet cake.

Cocoa Fudge Frosting

Combine in saucepan:

> ½ cup cocoa
> 1 cup confectioners' sugar
> 7 tablespoons milk
> ½ cup salted butter

Stir over medium heat just to boiling point. Remove from heat. Pour into mixing bowl.
Gradually add:

> 3 cups sifted confectioners' sugar

Beat to spreading consistency.
Stir in:

> 1 teaspoon vanilla

Fills and frosts two 8- or 9-inch layers.
For Cocoa Cake, page 15, sprinkle with:

> 1 cup chopped walnuts

Fudge Frosting

This is superlatively chocolaty and rich.
Bring to a boil in a large saucepan:

> 1 cup evaporated milk

Remove from the heat and in it dissolve, stirring:

> 2 cups granulated sugar
> ⅛ teaspoon salt
> 3 ounces grated unsweetened chocolate

Again bring to a boil, and cook without stirring to the soft ball stage (238° on a candy thermometer). Remove gently from the heat.
Cool to 110°.
Add:

4 tablespoons sweet butter
1 teaspoon vanilla

Beat to spreading consistency. Makes 2 cups.

Chocolate Mint Frosting

Over hot water in top of a double boiler, melt:

3 ounces unsweetened chocolate

in:

¾ cup evaporated milk
¼ cup water
1½ cups superfine granulated sugar

Stir until chocolate and milk are dissolved, then cook 30 minutes, stirring only occasionally.
Remove from heat.
Blend in:

¼ cup crème de menthe

Beat with rotary beater until smooth and spreadable. Makes 1 cup.

Instant Frosting

In a saucepan over hot, but not boiling, water, melt:

¼ cup sweet butter or margarine

Add:

1 cup instant chocolate mix
¼ cup milk (more or less depending on
    the chocolate product)

Heat mixture to boiling point, stirring constantly. *Do not boil.* Remove from heat. Pour into small mixer bowl.
Gradually add, beating until smooth:

2 cups confectioners' sugar
1 teaspoon vanilla

Spread frosting while warm. Frosts 30 cupcakes or one 13×9×2-inch cake.

Blended Frosting

Put the ingredients into a blender in the following order:

1 cup lukewarm evaporated milk
1½ teaspoons vanilla
1½ cups sugar
5 ounces unsweetened chocolate pieces
6 tablespoons sweet butter or margarine

Cover. Blend on medium speed until all pieces are chopped fine. Occasionally stop motor and stir. Blend at high speed until frosting becomes thick and creamy. Cool. Fills and frosts two 8-inch or 9-inch layers.

Walnut Condensed Milk Frosting

This frosting has a slight caramel taste which is particularly pleasant on a cocoa cake.

In top of a double boiler, over hot, but not boiling, water, melt:

3 ounces unsweetened chocolate with
15 ounces (1 can) sweetened condensed milk

Remove from the water and place over direct medium heat. Cook, stirring constantly, for 2½ minutes. Remove from the heat. Dip the pan in cold water to stop the caramelizing instantly. Cool a little. Fill the layers of the still warm cake with raspberry or cherry jam. Fold into the cooled frosting:

¾ cup chopped walnuts

Spread over the cake. Makes 1½ cups.

Simple Mocha Cocoa Frosting

To frost two 9-inch layers, cream well:

> ½ cup sweet butter

Sift together:

> 1 pound confectioners' sugar
> 3 tablespoons cocoa

Add alternately to the butter the dry ingredients and:

> ⅓ cup strong coffee
> 2 tablespoons vanilla

Beat until the sugar is completely dissolved, or about 8 minutes at medium speed.

Rich Chocolate Frosting

In a saucepan over hot, but not boiling, water, melt together:

> 2 cups semisweet chocolate pieces
> ¾ cup black coffee

Pour mixture into bowl. Beat in:

> 2 sticks sweet butter

cut into small pieces, one piece at a time. Continue beating until mixture is smooth.

Cover and frost 9-inch layer cake, or Cassata, page 39.

Chocolate Marshmallow Frosting

This is extremely sweet, very fluffy.

Melt in top of double boiler over simmering water:

> 3 ounces unsweetened chocolate

Add:

> 1 cup miniature or 10 large marshmallows

and stir until melted. Remove from heat and pour into small mixer bowl. On low speed of mixer, beat in:

> 1/4 cup sweet butter or margarine
> 1 teaspoon vanilla

Add alternately:

> 2½ cups confectioners' sugar

and:

> 1/4 cup milk

and beat until frosting is of spreading consistency. Fills and frosts two 8-inch or 9-inch layers.

Creme Patissière, or Custard Filling

Scald:

> 2 cups milk

Dissolve:

> 3 tablespoons cornstarch in
> 1/4 cup cold water

Soften:

> 1 tablespoon granulated gelatin in
> 4 tablespoons cold water

Beat in the top of a quart-size double boiler:

> 2 eggs
> 1/3 cup sugar

over boiling water. Pour the scalded milk over the eggs, stir in the cornstarch and the gelatin, and cook the cream until it thickens enough to coat the spoon. Use as a filling for profiteroles, cream puffs, éclairs, etc.
For a richer filling, fold in 1 cup whipped cream when lukewarm or when the gelatin is just about to set. Makes 2½ cups.

Chocolate Custard Filling

Scald:

> 1½ cups milk

Melt in it:

> 2 ounces unsweetened chocolate

Reserve. In a saucepan, beat together:

> ½ cup granulated sugar
> 4 egg yolks

until creamy and light-colored. Add:

> ¼ cup cornstarch

mixing just enough to blend. Over medium heat pour the chocolate mixture gradually into the egg mixture, stirring continually and rapidly until it reaches the boiling point and coats the spoon. Remove at once from the heat. Add:

> 1 teaspoon vanilla

Cool, stirring occasionally to prevent a skin from forming. This is a filling for éclairs, puffs, and pies. Makes 2 cups.

Blended Mocha Butter Cream

Grate:

> 2 ounces semisweet chocolate pieces

Cover and blend at high speed for 6 seconds.
Scrape the chocolate away from sides with a rubber spatula.
Add:

> 6 tablespoons triple-strength cold
> black coffee

Cover and blend 6 seconds.
Add:

> 1 cup confectioners' sugar
> 4 egg yolks
> 1 stick sweet butter, softened

Blend 15 seconds.
If too runny, chill to spreading consistency. Makes 1 cup, enough for a
3-layer cake. Use filling of your choice.

Blended Chocolate Butter Cream

Grate:

> 6 ounces semisweet chocolate pieces

in the blender. Cover and blend at high speed for 6 seconds.
Scrape the ground chocolate away from the sides with a rubber spatula.
Add:

> ¼ cup cold coffee

Cover and blend 6 more seconds. Add:

> 4 tablespoons confectioners' sugar
> 4 egg yolks
> 1 stick sweet butter, softened
> 2 tablespoons Cognac

Blend 15 seconds.
If runny, chill to spreading consistency. Makes 1 cup, enough for a 3-layer
cake. Use filling of your choice.

French Mocha Butter Cream

In a saucepan over hot, but not boiling water, melt:

> 2 ounces unsweetened chocolate

In another pan combine:

> 1 cup granulated sugar
> ⅓ cup water

Heat, stirring, to 238° on a candy thermometer, or until the syrup spins a thread. Beat:

> **5 egg yolks**

until thick and pale.
Gradually add the syrup, while continuing to beat. Cool.
Beat into the mixture:

> **1¼ sticks salted butter**

and the melted chocolate. Add:

> **3 tablespoons each of Cointreau and instant coffee**

Makes 2 cups.

Low Calorie Whipped Topping

To:

> **½ cup water**

Add:

> **2½ tablespoons sugar**
> **1 teaspoon vanilla**
> **1 tablespoon sifted cocoa**
> **½ cup nonfat dry milk**

Beat together until stiff, about 15 minutes. Chill. Makes 1 cup.
Will cover a dessert for 6.
150 calories per recipe.

Orange Topping

Blend:

> **3 tablespoons orange juice**
> **2 tablespoons melted sweet butter or margarine**

Stir into:

> 2 cups sifted confectioners' sugar

until smooth.
Add:

> 1 teaspoon grated orange peel

Pour over top of cake. Makes 1 cup.

Honey Topping

Cream together:

> ¾ cup honey
> ½ cup softened sweet butter
> ¼ cup cocoa

Pour over the top of cake. Makes 1 cup.

Almond Fluff Topping

In a chilled bowl, combine:

> 1 cup sifted confectioners' sugar
> 2 cups heavy cream
> ½ cup sifted cocoa
> Dash salt
> ½ teaspoon almond extract

Beat until the topping holds a peak.
Fold in:

> ½ cup toasted blanched slivered almonds

reserving some for garnish. Makes 4½ cups.

Cherry Topping

Beat together:

> ½ cup sifted confectioners' sugar
> 1 stiffly beaten egg white

Add:

> dash of salt
> ½ teaspoon almond extract
> ¼ cup chopped, well drained maraschino
> cherries, reserving a few for garnish

Spoon onto cake.
Garnish with reserved cherries.
Makes ¾ cup.

Chocolate Cinnamon-Flecked Topping

Fold:

> 1 teaspoon cinnamon
> ¼ cup grated sweet chocolate

into:

> 1 cup whipped cream

For decorating upside-down fruit cakes, use large dollops or rosettes made with a pastry tube, allowing the fruit to show.

Minted Topping

Combine:

> 1½ cups heavy cream
> ½ cup instant chocolate mix

⅛ teaspoon salt
few drops peppermint extract

Beat until stiff, glossy peaks form. Fill cake. Frost top and sides. Chill several hours or overnight. Decorate with rows of colored mint fondant or crushed candy cane. Makes 3½ cups.

Prune and Nut Filling for Chocolate Cake

Chop:

1 cup pitted cooked prunes

Mix well with:

⅓ cup orange marmalade
⅓ cup chopped pecans
1 teaspoon lemon juice

Spread between layers. Frost the cake with Rich Chocolate Frosting, page **68.**

Cookies

Making cookies is fun. It's even more fun when good friends make them together. To be successful, grease baking sheets (when the recipe calls for it) with peanut oil, margarine, sweet butter, or any other *unsalted* fat. Do not use corn oil; the sugars in it brown the baking sheets.

The best cookies sheets are those with a permanently shiny baking surface and a dull bottom. They produce a more even baking. Always place the shallow pans for bars and squares and the baking sheets for cookies 2 inches from the oven walls, and bake only on one rack of the oven. The baking pan or baking sheet should be washed with cold water if it is to be reused for the second batch, or cookies will spread before baking. The appearance of cookies is enhanced by dusting granulated sugar or grated chocolate over them before baking.

Cookie cutters come in a great variety. I prefer those with fluted edges. Checkerboard and striped patterns can be designed by slicing and rearranging cuts of light and dark dough. Strips of dough can be coiled, twisted, pinched, and recombined into any shape. Imprinting the surface of the cookies can be done with a fork, nuts, bolts, heavy rope, any clean textured object.

Icebox cookies are quicker to make than rolled ones. After mixing the dough, shape into a 2½-inch-diameter roll. Wrap it well in foil. Chill or freeze. Then slice and bake.

For variations, roll the entire roll in nuts. Chocolate and yellow dough may be rolled together to form pinwheels.

Rolled cookies are best when rolled between two sheets of plastic wrap. Peel off the plastic on one side. Place on the board, plastic side down, and cut with a floured cutter. Roll the remaining dough between fresh plastic.

Cookies freeze very well. Put them in Baggies and keep the Baggies in plastic containers to avoid breakage. Cookies may be stored in cookie jars for short periods. Buttery cookies should be kept in the refrigerator since they become rancid in kitchen temperatures. Squares may be stored right in the pan, covered with aluminum foil.

Brownies

Preheat oven to 325°.
Beat:

6 eggs

until thick and lemon-colored. Add:

3 cups granulated sugar

¼ cup at a time, beating thoroughly after each addition.
Reserve.
Place in a pan:

6 ounces unsweetened chocolate

Cover with boiling water and allow to stand until soft. Pour off all the hot water. Into the melted chocolate, quickly stir:

¼ stick softened sweet butter

then add:

2 teaspoons vanilla

and beat into the reserved egg mixture. Sift together:

1½ cups flour
½ teaspoon salt

Add to the batter and beat until smooth. Fold in:

2 cups chopped walnuts

Pour into a greased 12×15-inch pan, and bake 25 to 30 minutes. Cut into fifty 2-inch squares.
May be frosted with Fudge Frosting, page 65, when cooled.

Chocolate Syrup Brownies

Preheat oven to 350°.
Cream together until light and fluffy:

> ½ cup sweet butter or margarine
> 1 cup granulated sugar

Add:

> 1 teaspoon vanilla

Add, one at a time, beating well after each addition:

> 2 eggs

Combine:

> 1½ cups all-purpose flour
> ¼ teaspoon baking soda

Add alternately to creamed mixture with:

> ¾ cup chocolate syrup

Stir in:

> ¾ cup chopped pecans

Pour into a greased 9×9×2-inch pan. Bake for 40 to 45 minutes or until done.
Makes 16 brownies, which may be frosted with Fudge Frosting, page 65.

Chocolate Cream Cheese Brownies

Preheat oven to 350°.
Blend:

> ¾ cup sweet butter or margarine
> 1 package (3 ounces) cream cheese,
>   softened

Add gradually:

> 1 cup granulated sugar

Cream until light and fluffy.
Beat in:

1 egg
1 teaspoon vanilla

In a saucepan over hot, but not boiling, water, melt:

> 2 cups semisweet chocolate pieces
> ¼ cup sweet butter or margarine

Stir to blend. Combine melted chocolate with creamed mixture.
Sift:

> 2½ cups sifted all-purpose flour
> 1 teaspoon baking powder

Gradually add to creamed mixture until well blended.
Spoon into a greased 13×9×2-inch pan and sprinkle with:

> ½ cup chopped nuts

Bake about 30 minutes. Makes 24 brownies.

Bran Brownies

Preheat oven to 350°.
In a saucepan over hot, but not boiling, water, melt:

> 2 ounces unsweetened chocolate

In a large bowl, cream:

> 1 cup sweet butter
> 1 cup granulated sugar

Add:

> 2 eggs
> melted chocolate
> ½ cup bran
> ⅓ cup all-purpose flour
> ½ teaspoon salt

Beat again.
Blend in:

> 1 teaspoon vanilla

Pour in 8×8-inch greased pan. Bake 45 minutes.

Graham Cracker Brownies

Preheat oven to 400°. Mix together:

> 20 graham crackers, rolled into crumbs
> ½ teaspoon baking powder
> 1 egg
> 1 can condensed milk
> 6 ounces semisweet chocolate pieces
> ⅓ cup chopped nuts
> 1 tablespoon grated orange rind

Pour into a 9-inch square greased pan. Bake 25 to 30 minutes. Cut in squares before cooling on a rack.

Chocolate Walnut Squares

Preheat oven to 350°.
In a saucepan over hot, but not boiling, water, melt:

> 1 ounce unsweetened chocolate
> 4 tablespoons sweet butter

Mix well.
Beat until thick:

> 2 eggs

Add:

> 1 cup granulated sugar

a little at a time, beating well after each addition with an egg beater or a wire whisk. Add this very slowly to the chocolate, beating briskly until batter is smooth and pale.
Beat in:

> 1 teaspoon vanilla
> ¼ cup light cream
> ½ teaspoon powdered cinnamon

Stir in:

> 1 cup twice-sifted cake flour

Mix with:

> ¼ teaspoon salt
> 1 cup chopped walnuts

Pour the batter into a greased 8-inch square pan. Bake about 30 minutes or until the top is firm. Cut into squares before removing the pan to the cooling rack.

Congo Squares

Preheat oven to 350°.
In a saucepan over hot, but not boiling, water, melt:

> ⅔ cup salted butter

Remove from heat and stir in:

> 2¼ cups brown sugar
> 1 teaspoon vanilla

Transfer mixture to large mixing bowl. Allow to cool.
Sift together:

> 2¾ cups sifted cake flour
> 2½ teaspoons baking powder
> ¼ teaspoon salt

Add, one at a time:

> 3 eggs

to the cooled sugar mixture, beating well after each addition. Stir in dry ingredients. Then add:

> 1 cup chopped nuts
> 1 cup semisweet chocolate pieces

Spread in a greased 13×9×2-inch pan. Bake 25 to 30 minutes. When almost cool, cut into 2-inch squares.

Pecan Squares

Preheat oven to 350°.
Sift together in a bowl:

> 1 cup all-purpose flour
> ½ teaspoon baking powder
> ¼ teaspoon salt

Cut in:

> ½ stick sweet butter, softened

with pastry blender until the mixture is in fine crumbs. Pat evenly into a well-greased 9-inch square pan. Bake 15 minutes.
Meanwhile, in a saucepan, over hot, but not boiling, water, melt:

> 1 cup semisweet chocolate pieces

Remove from the heat. Combine in a bowl:

> ½ cup brown sugar, well packed
> 2 eggs
> ¼ cup corn syrup
> 1½ teaspoons vanilla
> ¼ teaspoon salt

Beat thoroughly. Gradually add melted chocolate, stirring quickly. Stir in:

> ¼ cup chopped nuts

Pour evenly over partly baked batter. Sprinkle with:

> ¼ cup chopped nuts

Bake for 25 minutes more. Cut into thirty-six 1½-inch squares while warm. Cool.

Feezies

Invented by a lady named Fee, these make a good dessert served right from the oven, topped with whipped cream.

Preheat oven to 325°.

Cream together:

> ½ cup sweet butter
> 1 cup brown sugar, well packed
> ¼ cup cocoa
> 1 cup sifted all-purpose flour
> 1 teaspoon salt
> 1¼ cups oatmeal, uncooked

Press half of this mixture ¼ inch thick into a buttered 9-inch pan.
Boil together until soft:

> ½ pound pitted dates
> ½ cup lemon juice
> ½ cup water
> 1 teaspoon grated lime peel

Spread this over the oatmeal mixture in the pan. Cover with remaining oatmeal mixture, and dot with:

> 2 tablespoons sweet butter

Bake 45 minutes. While still warm cut into squares.

Czechoslovak Chocolate Perniky

These are old-fashioned chewy cakes.

Preheat oven to 350°.
Sift together three times:

> 3 cups all-purpose flour
> ½ cup granulated sugar
> 3 tablespoons cocoa
> 1 teaspoon baking soda
> ¼ teaspoon mace
> ½ teaspoon cloves
> ¼ teaspoon allspice
> 1 teaspoon cinnamon

Make a well with the dry ingredients; place in it:

> 1 beaten egg
> 1¼ cups lukewarm honey

(Be sure to warm the honey over very low heat.)

> 3 tablespoons salted butter
> 3 tablespoons milk

Work into a smooth dough. Let stand in a warm place, covered with plastic, overnight. It will rise slightly due to the honey. Roll to ½-inch thickness. Spread in a greased 13×9×2-inch pan. Bake for 25 to 30 minutes. Cut into squares.

These keep forever.

Chocolate Shortbread

Preheat oven to 300°.

In a large bowl place:

> 2 sticks sweet butter, softened
> ½ cup superfine granulated sugar
> ¼ cup cocoa
> 1¾ cups all-purpose flour

With your hands, work until the dough becomes like clay. Put into a 10-inch springmold. Prick around the edges with a fork for decoration, and with a knife score into 12 wedges.

Bake 30 to 40 minutes. While still hot, cut the wedges. When cold, store in airtight container.

Chocolate Wafers

Preheat oven to 400°.

In a large mixing bowl, cream together until light:

> ¾ cup sweet butter
> 1¼ cups granulated sugar

Add, beating well:

> ¼ cup dark rum
> 1 egg

Sift together:

> 1½ cups sifted all-purpose flour
> ¾ cup cocoa
> 1½ teaspoons baking powder
> ¼ teaspoon salt

Add the dry ingredients gradually to the first mixture, beating after each addition.

Roll the dough out ⅛ inch thick on a lightly floured board. Cut with a floured cookie cutter into rounds about 2½ inches in diameter. Dust with crystallized sugar and press lightly into the dough. Bake the rounds on an ungreased baking sheet for 8 minutes. Makes 18 to 24 wafers.

Chocolate Snaps

These are crisp cookies.

Preheat oven to 350°.
Grate:

> 2 ounces unsweetened chocolate

Sift together:

> 1 cup flour
> 1 teaspoon baking powder

Beat until stiff:

> 8 egg whites

Beat in gradually:

> 2 cups confectioners' sugar

to make a stiff meringue. Fold in grated chocolate, sifted flour mixture, and:

> 2 teaspoons grated orange peel

Drop batter by teaspoons 2 inches apart on a buttered baking sheet. Bake the cookies 8 to 10 minutes. Makes 24 to 36 cookies.

Chocolate Fedoras

Preheat oven to 450°.
Beat:

> 3 egg whites

until they are stiff, with:

> ½ teaspoon vanilla

Sift together:

> ¼ cup powdered almonds
> ¼ cup powdered hazelnuts
> ½ cup granulated sugar
> 1 tablespoon sifted all-purpose flour

Add this to the egg whites, cutting and folding it in with a metal spatula.
Roll out to ¼-inch thickness on floured board.
Cut cookies the size of half-dollars, with an oval cutter.
Bake on a buttered and floured baking sheet 4 or 5 minutes or until lightly browned. Remove from the pan before they cool.
When cool, pair and fill with Fudge Frosting, page 65. Makes 24 cookies.

Chocolate Coconut Kisses

Preheat the oven to 275°.
In a saucepan, over hot, but not boiling, water, melt:

> 4 ounces semisweet chocolate

Meanwhile, beat:

> 3 egg whites

until they stand in glossy peaks.
Sift over the egg whites:

> 1 tablespoon all-purpose flour

Fold in:

> ¾ cup dried coconut flakes
> 1 cup sifted confectioners' sugar

Fold the melted chocolate into the foamy mixture. Drop from teaspoon on waxed paper on cookie sheet. Bake 30 to 35 minutes. Makes 3 dozen.

Chocolate Oatmeal Cookies

Preheat oven to 375°.
Cream:

> ½ cup sweet butter or margarine, softened
> ⅓ cup granulated sugar
> ⅓ cup brown sugar, well packed

Add until mixed together:

> 1 egg, well beaten
> ½ teaspoon vanilla

Sift together:

> ¾ cup all-purpose flour
> ½ teaspoon salt
> 1 teaspoon baking powder

Add alternately to butter mixture with:

> ¼ cup milk

Stir in:

> ½ cup chopped nuts (your choice)
> 1½ cups rolled oats
> 1 cup semisweet chocolate pieces

Drop by teaspoons onto a lightly greased baking sheet.
Bake 10 to 12 minutes. About 4 dozen cookies.

Oatmeal Chocolate Chip Cookies

Preheat oven to 400°.
In a large bowl, cream together:

> 2 sticks salted butter
> 2 cups brown sugar, well packed

Beat in:

>2 eggs
>1 teaspoon vanilla
>¼ cup heavy cream

On waxed paper, sift:

>2½ cups all-purpose flour
>1 teaspoon salt
>1 teaspoon baking soda

and mix into the creamed mixture. Add:

>2 cups quick-cooking oatmeal
>1 cup chopped walnuts
>2 cups semisweet chocolate pieces

and mix well. Drop from a teaspoon, about 2 inches apart, onto a greased cookie sheet. Bake 10 to 12 minutes. Makes 5 dozen cookies.

Swiss Almond Cookies

Preheat the oven to 400°.
In a bowl mix thoroughly:

>¾ cup grated almonds
>⅔ cup granulated sugar
>3 egg yolks

In another bowl, sift together:

>1 cup flour
>¼ cup cocoa

and make a well in the center. Put the almond mixture into the well, then add:

>2 tablespoons soft salted butter
>½ teaspoon salt
>1 teaspoon vanilla
>1 teaspoon almond extract

Work all the ingredients into a firm dough and chill 1 hour. Roll out the dough to ⅛-inch thickness on a lightly floured board and cut into 1-inch rounds with a floured cookie cutter.

Beat:

> **1 egg yolk**
> **1 teaspoon cold water**

Brush the cookies with this mixture. Sprinkle with a mixture of:

> **½ cup slivered blanched almonds**
> **¼ cup granulated sugar**

Bake 8 to 10 minutes on a greased cookie sheet. Makes 24 cookies.

Chocolate Icebox Cookies

These cookies are buttery and rich, but not too sweet.

Preheat oven to 350°.
In a saucepan, over hot, but not boiling, water, melt:

> **4 ounces unsweetened chocolate**

In a large bowl, cream:

> **2 sticks sweet butter**
> **1 cup granulated sugar**

Add the melted chocolate and:

> **1 egg**
> **6 tablespoons heavy cream**
> **1 teaspoon vanilla**

Beat thoroughly. Sift together:

> **3 cups sifted flour**
> **1 teaspoon cinnamon**
> **3 teaspoons baking powder**
> **½ teaspoon salt**

and mix the dry ingredients into the egg mixture. Fold in:

> **1 cup chopped nuts**

and mix well. Shape the dough into a sausage; slice crosswise to ⅛ inch thick. Bake 10 to 12 minutes. Makes 5 dozen cookies.

Bodensee Möpsli

A famous Swiss dessert.

Form:

> 1 recipe Icebox Cookies, above

into a roll 2 inches in diameter. Roll in:

> **granulated sugar**

Bake according to directions. Spread:

> **¼ inch cherry, raspberry, or apricot jam**

between 2 cookies. Put pairs on a rack and ice top and sides with:

> **Italian Meringue, page 59**

to look like a snowball. Sprinkle with chocolate shot or curls.

Mandelbrot

These almond cookies are very light in texture.

Preheat oven to 325°. Beat:

> **3 eggs**
> **¾ cup granulated sugar**

until the mixture is light-colored and thick. Add:

> **1 tablespoon orange juice**
> **1 teaspoon grated orange peel**
> **1 teaspoon almond extract**

Sift:

> **2¾ cups flour**
> **2 teaspoons double-acting baking powder**

Fold half the flour into the egg mixture with:

> **6 tablespoons peanut oil**

Add the remaining flour and beat for 30 seconds. To ¼ of the dough add:

> **½ cup chopped blanched almonds**
> **4 tablespoons cocoa**

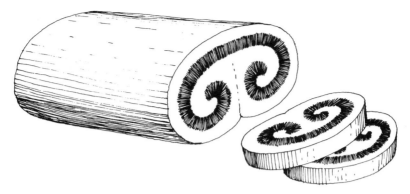

Form the almond cocoa dough into a double roll as illustrated.

Roll out the remaining dough to ½-inch thickness and wrap around the cocoa roll. Seal with a few drops of water where the double rolls meet.

If the roll is too long, cut in half. Place on a greased baking sheet. Bake 30 minutes. Remove from the oven. Cool.

Make slices ½ inch thick, place them on greased baking sheets and bake again 5 minutes. The almond swirls look pretty in the center of the two-tone cookie.

Berliner Brot

Preheat oven to 350°. In a saucepan over hot, but not boiling, water, melt:

> 1½ ounces semisweet chocolate

Beat lightly:

> 3 small eggs

with:

> 1½ cups brown sugar, well packed

Add melted chocolate. Sift together:

> ½ teaspoon cinnamon
> ½ teaspoon allspice
> ½ teaspoon baking powder
> 1 cup all-purpose flour

Add dry ingredients alternately to the creamed mixture with:

> 2 tablespoons milk

Add:

> ½ cup chopped almonds

and stir until the dough is well blended. Spread ½ inch thick in 13×9×2-inch pans. Bake only one panful at a time in the middle of the oven for 25 minutes. Cut in bars or squares. Cool on a rack. When cold, brush tops with 1 recipe of Royal Icing, page 63. Makes 50 cookies.

Caramel Oat Bars

Preheat oven to 350°.
In a bowl combine:

> ½ cup softened sweet butter
> ½ cup sugar

Beat until creamy. Add:

> ¾ cup sifted flour
> ¾ cup rolled oats
> 1 teaspoon vanilla
> ½ teaspoon salt

Mix to blend. Press evenly into ungreased 13×9×1-inch pan. Bake 12 to 15 minutes. Meanwhile, combine over hot, but not boiling, water:

> 1 cup semisweet chocolate pieces
> ⅓ cup corn syrup
> 2 tablespoons sweet butter
> 1 teaspoon vanilla
> ¼ teaspoon salt

Stir until smooth. Stir in:

> 1 cup chopped walnuts

Cool. Spread over cookie base. Cut into 4 dozen 2×1-inch bars.

French Chocolate Macaroons

These macaroons are chewy and soft on the inside when fresh.

Preheat oven to 350°.
Beat:

with:

  3 **egg whites**

  ¾ **cup granulated sugar**

Add:

  1 **cup slivered almonds**

Stir in:

  4 **ounces melted sweet chocolate pieces**
  2 **teaspoons almond extract**
  3 **unbeaten egg whites**

Blend thoroughly and drop the dough by the teaspoon on a greased cookie sheet. Bake 15 minutes.

 Cool the macaroons before removing from the pan. Makes 18 to 24 macaroons.

Macaroons à l 'Haïtienne

Preheat oven to 350°. Beat:

  4 **egg whites**

until they hold soft peaks. Add:

  1 **teaspoon vanilla**

Gradually beat in:

  1 **cup confectioners' sugar**

and continue beating until the mixture is stiff and glossy. Fold in:

  ⅓ **cup all-purpose flour**
  2 **cups dried grated coconut**

Drop by teaspoons 1 inch apart on a greased and floured baking sheet. Bake 15 minutes.

FILLING:

Flavor:

  1 **recipe Chocolate Butter Cream, page 71**

by adding:

  1 **jigger rum**

with the last strokes of the beater. Join two macaroons with ¼-inch filling between the undersides. Makes 18 to 24 macaroons.

Florentines

Preheat oven to 350°.
Sift:

> ⅓ cup flour

Sift again to measure ⅓ cup exactly.
Add:

> ⅛ teaspoon salt
> ¼ teaspoon soda

Sift once more.
Cream:

> ¼ cup salted butter
> ⅓ cup firmly packed brown sugar

until light and fluffy.
Add:

> 2 tablespoons corn syrup
> 1 egg

Beat well.
Stir in the dry ingredients with:

> ½ teaspoon vanilla
> ½ cup dried coconut flakes

Drop from a teaspoon, about 2 inches apart, on a greased baking sheet. Spread into thin rounds. Bake about 10 minutes.
Remove at once from the baking sheet, *working fast*. If the cookies are not removed fast they will break. Cool.
Melt over hot, not boiling, water:

> 2 ounces sweet chocolate

Drip the chocolate in a lacy pattern over the cookies.
Let them stand several hours or until the chocolate is firm.
Makes 4 dozen cookies.

Chocolate Peanut Butter Drops

Preheat oven to 375°.
Sift together:

>1½ cups sifted all-purpose flour
>½ teaspoon baking powder
>¼ teaspoon baking soda
>½ teaspoon salt

Cream:

>⅓ cup sweet butter or margarine
>¾ cup creamy peanut butter

Gradually blend in:

>½ cup granulated sugar
>½ cup brown sugar

Add:

>1 teaspoon vanilla
>1 egg, well beaten

Mix thoroughly. Stir in the flour mixture with:

>½ cup milk

Mix well.
Fold in:

>1 cup semisweet chocolate pieces
>½ cup chopped salted peanuts

Drop by teaspoonfuls onto ungreased baking sheet. Bake for 8 to 10 minutes. Makes about 4 dozen cookies.

Translucent Cookies

These cookies look like stained glass windows. They make wonderful Christmas gifts. This dough, rolled out and cut with a cookie cutter, could also be used for plain cookies.

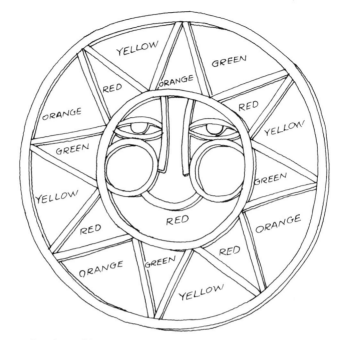

In a large bowl, combine:

> ⅓ cup corn oil
> 1 cup firmly packed dark brown sugar
> 1½ cups blackstrap molasses

Blend thoroughly.
Mix with:

> ⅔ cup water

Sift together on waxed paper:

> 5¾ cups all-purpose flour
> 2 teaspoons baking soda
> 1 teaspoon salt
> ½ teaspoon cinnamon
> ¼ teaspoon nutmeg
> 1 tablespoon dried powdered orange peel
> ½ cup cocoa

Beat the dry ingredients into the first mixture a little at a time.
Divide the dough in balls and with the palm of the hand roll very thin into 12-inch strips.
Cut two layers of waxed paper to fit a cookie sheet.
With the strips of dough make outlines on the waxed paper as illustrated, or of birds or butterflies.

With a mortar and pestle or a rolling pin, crush coarsely:

> 1 pound sour balls of different colors
> (each color separately)

Place different colors in the open areas of each bird or butterfly.
Bake on the paper 3 to 6 minutes, depending on the melting properties
of the candy. When cool enough to be handled, remove from the paper.
Place on a rack until cold. Wrap unused cookies individually in wax paper
or Saran. Store in dry place in airtight containers. Makes 20 to 26 two-inch
cookies.

Chocolate Fleck Rings

Preheat oven to 350°. Mix together to a smooth and soft dough:

> 2 sticks sweet butter
> 1 cup granulated sugar
> 2 cups all-purpose flour
> ⅛ teaspoon salt
> 3 tablespoons finely chopped almonds
> 4 egg yolks
> 2 ounces grated sweet chocolate

Add:

> 1 tablespoon grated lemon peel
> 1 tablespoon cinnamon

When the dough is thoroughly mixed to blend, roll it out ⅛ inch thick on a
floured pastry board and cut with a two-inch ring cookie cutter. Place the
rings on a buttered baking sheet and brush with slightly beaten egg white.
Bake 10 to 15 minutes.

VARIATION:

This dough may also be used for apricot or raspberry filled cookies.
Cut as many cookie rounds as rings. Brush thinly with jam. Cover with
rings. Bake as above. While still hot, fill ring hole with fresh jam. Dust the
ring only with cocoa and confectioners' sugar in even parts.
Makes 36 rings or 18 filled cookies.

Belgian Christmas Rings

Preheat oven to 350°.
Sift:

> 3 cups all-purpose flour
> 1 teaspoon baking soda

Place in a large bowl and add:

> 1 cup softened sweet butter
> 1 cup lukewarm honey (warm over very
>   low heat)
> 4 egg yolks
> ½ cup cocoa
> ½ cup granulated sugar
> 2 tablespoons grated almonds
> 1 teaspoon grated orange rind
> 1 teaspoon cinnamon

Combine and work together (use your hands) until the dough feels and looks like clay. Roll out on a floured board to ⅛-inch thickness and cut out with a floured one-inch ring cutter. Place rings on greased baking sheet. Brush with:

> 1 beaten egg white

Sprinkle with green and red colored sugar. Bake for 10 to 15 minutes. Makes 36 rings.

Nürnberger Lebkuchen

Wonderful German Christmas cookies.

Preheat oven to 325°. In the large bowl of an electric mixer, beat:

> 2 eggs
> ⅞ cup granulated sugar

until light-colored and thick.
Mix together:

1½ cups ground almonds
1½ cups ground hazelnuts
⅛ teaspoon cloves
1 teaspoon cinnamon
2 teaspoons grated orange rind
3 tablespoons cocoa

Fold into the egg mixture, then with wet hands roll into 24 balls. Place 1½ inches apart on a greased baking sheet and bake 17 minutes.
Frost the cookies while warm with:

Glossy Chocolate Icing, page 61

Rum Balls

Crush:

24 vanilla wafers

Place the crumbs in a bowl with:

1 cup finely chopped pecans
1 cup superfine granulated sugar
2 tablespoons cocoa
⅓ cup rum
1 tablespoon honey

and mix all ingredients. Drop from a teaspoon onto a baking sheet and chill. On waxed paper, roll into marble-size balls. Sift together:

½ cup confectioners' sugar
1 teaspoon cinnamon

Mix in:

1 teaspoon grated lime peel

Roll the balls in the mixture and let them stand until the sugar is partially absorbed; roll in the sugar mixture once more. Store between layers of waxed paper in an airtight container.

VARIATION:

Substitute ⅓ cup bourbon for the rum in the recipe above. Makes 24 balls.

Chocolate Leaves

This is the original recipe from La Marquise de Sévigné, one of Paris's most elegant chocolate shops. Almond paste can be purchased at gourmet sections of department stores.

Preheat oven to 350°.
Add:

> 1 cup almond paste to
> 2 unbeaten egg whites

and blend until smooth. Sift:

> ¾ cup presifted confectioners' sugar
> ⅓ teaspoon salt
> 4 tablespoons all-purpose flour

Combine with first mixture.
Form the leaves with a special leaf-shaped metal stencil (or form a wire leaf and cut and lift from patted-out batter).
Place on buttered cookie sheet. Bake 10 minutes. Remove from the pan while still hot. Coat with:

> Hard Chocolate Icing, page 61

Makes 18 leaves.

Madeleines au Chocolat

Preheat oven to 425°. Butter molds and lightly dust with 1 teaspoon cornstarch, shaking off all excess.

Beat:

> 2 egg yolks

with:

> ½ cup powdered sugar
> ¼ cup Dutch process cocoa

for 2 minutes.

Sift:

> ½ cup cake flour
> 1 teaspoon baking powder

then fold them into egg mixture.

Whisk:

> 2 egg whites

until stiff, then fill each shell of the mold ⅔ full. Bake 10 to 15 minutes.

Pastry

Pâte à Choux, or Basic Chou Paste

Pâte à Choux is a boiled pastry with the texture of popovers when baked. It is the easiest pastry to make and has many uses.

Preheat oven to 450°.
In a quart saucepan, place:

> **1 cup hot water**
> **1 stick salted butter**

Bring to a rolling boil over high heat, stirring often to melt the butter. Then add, all at one time:

> **2 cups all-purpose flour**

Reduce the heat. With a wooden spoon, stir vigorously for 2 minutes or until the mixture leaves the sides of the pan (it shrinks to form a lump). Remove from heat. Cool slightly and transfer to the large bowl of the electric mixer. Add:

> **9 eggs**

one at a time, beating each one into the batter for about 20 seconds or for one minute if beating by hand. Then beat the batter 2 minutes more, or 5 minutes if by hand.

Place in the refrigerator for 1 hour. Drop from a spoon on a greased baking sheet or use the plain nozzle of a pastry tube to make *choux* or hollow puffs. Bake for 12 minutes at 450°, then for 15 to 20 minutes at 350°. Makes:

> 30 profiterole-size choux, or
> 12 large dessert choux, or
> 18 medium éclairs, or
> 30 miniature éclairs

Éclairs Chantilly

Preheat oven to 450°.
Make one Basic Chou recipe.
With the widest plain nozzle of a pastry tube, spread pastry fingers 2 inches long on a greased cookie sheet.
Bake 12 minutes at 450°, then 15 to 20 minutes at 350°.
Cool.
When the éclairs are cold, slice the tops off and ice them with Éclair Glaze.

FILLING:

Whip:

> 1 cup heavy cream

with:

> 1 cup granulated sugar
> 1 teaspoon vanilla

Just before serving, fill the bottoms with whipped cream, and replace the iced tops on the éclairs. Éclairs may also be filled with:

> Crème Patissière, page 69
> Chocolate Custard Filling, page 70

Profiteroles au Chocolat

Preheat oven to 450°.
Make a Basic Chou Paste recipe. Place dough in pastry bag with 1-inch tip and squeeze 1½-inch dollops onto well-greased and floured baking sheet. Paint with:

> 1 beaten egg yolk

Bake 5 to 7 minutes. Turn heat to 375° and bake another 15 minutes. Cool on rack.
Squeeze a filling of Creme Patissière, page 69, with the plain nozzle of a pastry tube into the bottoms of the puffs.

SAUCE:

Put in a saucepan:

> ¼ pound semisweet cooking chocolate
> ½ to ¾ cup water
> ¼ cup Cognac

Bring slowly to a boil and cook until glossy.
To assemble, dip filled puffs in chocolate sauce. Place on serving dish, piling to resemble a pyramid. Pour remaining sauce over the top.

Rum Chocolate Puffs

Make 12 large puffs according to the Basic Chou Paste recipe, page 102. Cut the puffs across the top. Fill with:

> **Chocolate Custard Filling, page 70,**
> flavored with 1 jigger rum

Cover and dust with confectioners' sugar.

Chocolate Pancakes

Heat pancake griddle to 350°.
Beat:

>   4 egg yolks

until light and thick.
Beat in:

>   ¼ cup water
>   ¼ cup sifted flour
>   ¼ cup instant chocolate mix

Beat:

>   4 egg whites

until they hold glossy peaks. Add to mixture.
Brush the griddle with sweet butter. Drop chocolate mixture by tablespoons.
Fry until delicately brown on both sides, turning only once.
Serve with sour cherry preserves.

Chocolate Doughnuts

In a saucepan over hot, but not boiling, water, melt:

>   1½ ounces unsweetened chocolate

with:

>   2 tablespoons sweet butter

Cool. Meanwhile beat:

>   3 eggs

with:

>   1¼ cups granulated sugar
>   1 cup sour milk, page 12

Still beating, add the chocolate and butter mixture. Sift:

>   3¾ cups all-purpose flour

with:

>1 teaspoon soda
>2 teaspons baking powder
>½ teaspoon salt
>½ teaspoon nutmeg or mace

Add:

>1 teaspoon grated lemon peel

Blend the sifted ingredients into the egg mixture; beat a few strokes. Chill the dough for easier handling. Turn onto a lightly floured board, roll it out 1 inch thick, handling as little as possible, and cut into rounds with a floured doughnut cutter. Fry the doughnuts, a few at a time, in hot deep fat (390°). Turn them as they brown and rise to the top of the fat; keep turning until evenly browned. Drain the doughnuts on absorbent paper, cool, and dust with confectioners' sugar. Or you may want to gild the lily and glaze them with:

>Sweet Chocolate Glaze, page 62

Chocolate Popovers

Preheat the oven to 375°.
In a bowl, beat well:

>**2 eggs**
>**2 cups milk**
>**⅓ cup instant chocolate drink mix**
>**1 cup all-purpose flour**

Heat a black iron popover pan until the butter sizzles on it, then put:

>**1 teaspoon sweet butter in each popover cup**

and quickly brush it up the sides. Pour in the batter ⅔ full. Bake 40 to 45 minutes. Open the oven door. Dry the popovers in front of the oven 5 minutes. Meanwhile mix together a filling, Orange Cinnamon Flavored Sour Cream, page 133. Make a hole in the bottom of the popovers and put in a tablespoon of the filling instead of butter.

Bread Snacks

Bread and chocolate are traditionally combined in Europe as children's most beloved snack. In France the long loaves are cut crosswise, soft bread is pulled out of the crust and replaced with a chocolate bar. In Belgium, Holland, Austria, Switzerland, and Germany, sliced bread is well-buttered with sweet butter and a sandwich of chocolate sprinkles is enjoyed. In Spain and Italy, children are given almond-flavored fancy yeast breads soaked in chocolate milk which they spoon out of a bowl.

The following breads make more sophisticated snacks. The combination of bread and chocolate is always good.

Glazed Chocolate Chip Bread

Prepare one day ahead.

Preheat oven to 350°. Chop:

> **12 ounces semisweet chocolate pieces**

Combine in a bowl:

> **3 cups buttermilk biscuit mix**
> **¾ cup granulated sugar**

until there are no longer any large lumps.
Combine:

> **1 egg, slightly beaten**
> **¾ cup milk**
> **½ cup orange juice**

and add to dry ingredients. Beat vigorously by hand about one minute.
Add:

> **chopped chocolate pieces**
> **¾ cup walnuts**
> **1 tablespoon grated orange peel**

Spoon into well-greased 9×5×2¾-inch loaf pan. Bake 55 minutes or until done. Cool for 15 minutes in the pan, then cool on rack.
Store loaf tightly wrapped for one day to develop flavor. This loaf freezes well.
Before serving, glaze with:

> **½ recipe Viennese Chocolate Icing, page 63**

Chocolate Almond Loaf

A quick recipe.

Preheat oven to 350°. Separate:

> 1 package refrigerated flaky dinner rolls

into 18 sections. Arrange flat sides down in 3 rows on buttered 9×5×3-inch loaf pan (they will fill the pan when baked).
Mix:

> 3 tablespoons granulated sugar
> ¼ teaspoon cinnamon

Brush the rolls with:

> 1 tablespoon melted butter

Sprinkle with half the sugar mixture and:

> ⅛ cup slivered almonds
> ½ package semisweet chocolate bits

Separate the remaining rolls and cover the rolls in the pan. Again, sprinkle with remaining half of the sugar mixture and:

> ⅛ cup slivered almonds
> ½ package semisweet chocolate bits

Bake 20 to 25 minutes. Cool in the pan 5 minutes. Serve warm.

Pie Shells and Fillings

Pies to be served chilled should not be made of pastry. Cracker crumb shells chill well. Different effects are obtained when using zwieback crumbs, gingersnaps, vanilla or chocolate wafers, coconut or Brazil nuts to make a crust. Flavorings such as sesame seed, grated orange rind, cinnamon, and nutmeg combine well with chocolate fillings.

Experiment with shells and fillings and develop your "specialité de la maison" from these basic recipes.

Chocolate Vienna Pastry

Preheat oven to 450°.
Sift before measuring:

>¾ cup all-purpose flour
>¼ cup cocoa
>¼ teaspoon salt

Cut into the dry ingredients:

>1 stick sweet butter, softened
>4½ ounces cream cheese, softened

When well mixed, form into a ball. Wrap in foil. Chill 12 hours. When ready to use, roll to ⅛-inch thickness and place in a 9-inch pie pan. Bake for 12 minutes filled with dry rice or dry beans to prevent it from heaving. For tartlettes, form pastry over inverted muffin tins. Makes 6.

Chocolate Pastry Layer Cake

Use four layer-cake pans.

Preheat oven to 425°.
Shave:

>3 ounces sweet chocolate

Reserve.
In a small saucepan over hot, but not boiling, water, cook until smooth to make a sauce:

>5 ounces sweet chocolate
>½ cup sugar
>½ cup water
>½ teaspoon cinnamon

Remove from heat.
Add:

>2 teaspoons vanilla

Mix ¾ cup of this sauce into:

1 recipe Chocolate Vienna Pastry, page 109

Reserve the rest.

Divide into 4 dough balls. Put over the *outside* of 4 inverted layer cake pans, covering the bottom only. Bake 6 to 8 minutes. With a sharp knife trim any pastry that has spread over the edges.

Cool until firm—about 5 minutes. Carefully loosen the rounds from the pans.

Fold cool remaining sauce into:

2 cups whipped cream

Spread between and over top of stacked layers. Garnish with reserved shaved chocolate. Serve at once.

Crumb Pie Shell

Crush, then grind fine or put in a blender:

about 24 crackers, zwieback or wafers
making about 1½ cups of meal

Stir into this until well blended:

¼ cup sifted confectioners' sugar
or brown sugar, well packed

Flavor with:

1 teaspoon vanilla or other flavorings of
your choice

Pour evenly into a buttered 9-inch pie pan. Press another pie pan of the same size firmly into the crumbs. Remove the top pan and trim any excess which was forced over the edge. Bake 3 minutes in a 350° oven for a more "cooked" taste.

Scotch Cherry Pie

A jigger of whiskey does not hurt the flavor.

Preheat oven to 350°. Combine thoroughly:

> ¾ cup instant chocolate mix
> ½ cup uncooked oatmeal
> ¼ cup dried coconut flakes
> 1 tablespoon all-purpose flour
> ½ cup vanilla wafer crumbs
> (about 16 wafers)

Add:

> ¼ cup sweet butter or margarine, melted

Stir until ingredients are moistened (mixture should hold shape when pressed in hands).
Press crumbs firmly and evenly against bottom and sides of a 9-inch pie pan. Bake for 12 minutes.

FILLING:

Mix in a small saucepan:

> 3 tablespoons sugar
> 1½ teaspoons unflavored gelatin
> 1 cup cherry pie filling (from one 1 pound
> 6 ounce can)

Bring to boil over medium heat, stirring occasionally. Cook 1 minute to dissolve gelatin. Remove from heat.
Stir in:

> 2 tablespoons milk
> 1 tablespoon lemon juice
> ¼ teaspoon lemon extract

In a small mixer bowl whip at medium speed until smooth:

> 1 package (8 ounces) cream cheese

Reduce speed. Gradually add cherry mixture and blend well. Pour into pie shell. Refrigerate 2 hours or until firm.
Just before serving spread remaining 1½ cups cherry pie filling over top of cream cheese filling.

Chocolate Nut Crust

Use pecans, walnuts, almonds, hazelnuts, dried coconut flakes, or Brazil nuts.

Preheat oven to 375°.
Combine:

> 1 cup ground nuts
> 1 cup ground chocolate wafers
> ⅓ cup sweet butter

Press into 10-inch pie plate. Bake 7 minutes.

Chocolate Chiffon Pie

Combine in a saucepan:

> 1 tablespoon unflavored gelatin
> ½ cup granulated sugar
> ½ teaspoon salt

Stir in:

> 1¾ cups hot milk
> 1 cup semisweet chocolate pieces

Cook over medium heat, stirring constantly until chocolate melts and mixture appears smooth.
Remove from heat. Stir:

> ¼ cup of the hot mixture

into:

> 2 slightly beaten egg yolks

Return to saucepan and cook until mixture thickens. Remove from the heat at once. Add:

> 1 teaspoon vanilla

Pour into bowl. Place plastic wrap directly onto chocolate mixture.
Cool. Chill until partially set.

Remove from refrigerator and beat slightly until smooth. Beat:

2 egg whites

until foamy. Gradually add:

3 tablespoons sugar

and beat until stiff peaks form. Whip:

½ cup heavy cream

Fold beaten egg whites and whipped cream into cooled chocolate mixture.
Turn into prepared 9-inch pie shell.
Chill until firm. Just before serving, decorate with additional whipped
cream if desired.

Fudge Pie

Preheat oven to 325°.
Cream together:

1 stick salted butter
2 egg yolks

In a saucepan over hot, but not boiling, water, melt:

2 ounces unsweetened chocolate

Mix chocolate with egg yolks. Gradually add:

1 cup granulated sugar

Continue to beat.
Fold in:

⅓ cup sifted flour

Flavor with:

1 teaspoon vanilla

Then fold in:

2 egg whites, beaten until they hold
soft peaks

Bake in an 8-inch pie crust shell for 30 minutes. Serve the pie topped with
ice cream.

Brandy Black-Bottom Pie

This is one of the American South's contributions to haute cuisine.

Preheat oven to 300°.
Crush, then make crumbs from:

>48 gingersnaps

Knead with:

>1 stick sweet butter

Pat into 10-inch pie plate. Bake 5 minutes. Cool.
Soften:

>1 envelope unflavored gelatin

in:

>2 tablespoons water
>1 tablespoon brandy

Reserve for top filling.

BOTTOM FILLING:

Beat until light:

>4 egg yolks

Gradually add:

>½ cup dark brown sugar
>3¾ teaspoons cornstarch
>¼ teaspoon salt

Then stir in:

>1¼ cups milk
>5 tablespoons brandy

Cook this mixture in the top of a 2-quart double boiler over hot water until thick and smooth, beating constantly with a rotary or electric beater. Remove from the heat.
Melt:

>1½ squares unsweetened chocolate

in a bowl by covering with:

>2 cups boiling water

for three minutes, then quickly pour off the water. Stir one-half of the hot custard into the softened chocolate. Cool the chocolate custard, and pour into pie shell.

TOP FILLING:

Add reserved gelatin to rest of hot custard, mixing well.
Cool mixture slightly in refrigerator, but remove before it sets. Beat until stiff:

>4 egg whites
>¼ teaspoon cream of tartar

and beat in:

>1 teaspoon vanilla

Fold egg white mixture into cooled yellow custard. Pour this over chocolate filling in pie shell. Chill the pie at least 3 hours. Sprinkle with:

>½ cup shaved sweet chocolate

Beat:

>½ cup heavy cream
>1 teaspoon vanilla

With a pastry tube, make a border of whipped cream around the outer rim of the well-chilled pie. Serves 8.

Chocolate Banana Pie

In a large bowl, cream together:

>1 stick sweet butter
>1½ cups sifted confectioners' sugar

Add:

>2 eggs

Beat well after each addition. Whip:

>½ cup heavy cream

gradually adding:

>¼ cup granulated sugar
>2 teaspoons cocoa

Fold the cream into the large bowl mixture. Fold in:

> 1 cup chopped walnuts
> ¼ cup chopped maraschino cherries

Mash with a fork until they are smooth and glossy:

> 2 ripe bananas

with:

> 1 tablespoon lemon juice

Fold into the cream. Chill in 9-inch graham cracker pie crust. Decorate with shaved chocolate.

Chicago Grasshopper Pie

Invented by a lady who loved grasshopper cocktails.

Make Chocolate Nut Crust, page 112.
Fill with:

> ½ recipe Dark Chocolate Bavarian,
> page 145

Top with 1½ cups whipped cream flavored with:

> 1 ounce green crème de menthe
> 1 ounce crème de cacao

Decorate with chocolate curls.

Cocoa Cheese Pie

Preheat oven to 375°. Cream together:

> 16 ounces cream cheese
> 1 cup granulated sugar
> ½ cup cocoa
> 1 teaspoon vanilla

Beat in:

> 2 eggs

Continue beating until the mixture is thoroughly combined.

Fill a 9-inch graham cracker crust and bake for 20 minutes. Remove from oven and let cool 15 minutes.

Heat oven to 425°.

Combine:

> 1 cup sour cream
> 2 tablespoons superfine granulated sugar
> 1 teaspoon vanilla

Spread evenly over baked filling. Return the pie to the oven for 10 minutes. Chill overnight. Makes 10 to 12 servings.

Other CHILLED PIE FILLINGS for graham cracker crusts or meringue pie shells:

Soft Chocolate Custard, page 136

Swiss Chocolate Mousse, page 151

Rum Chipolata, page 137

Cherry Chocolate Fool, page 140

Light Chocolate Bavarian, page 144

Dark Chocolate Bavarian, page 145

Steamed and Baked Puddings

Modern steamed puddings are as light as a soufflé in texture. Served flaming with a spectacular sauce, they may be made two days ahead of a party. Stored in a mold in the freezer, they need only be reheated in a hot water bath for one hour before serving. Never use stale bread for puddings.

There are special molds, good also for bombes, with tight fitting lids. Without the lids you can use them for gelatin desserts. Coffee cans do well as a substitute but are more difficult to unmold. Butter the mold well with sweet butter or margarine. Place the mold on a trivet in a large pot with water ⅓ up the sides of the mold or can to let the steam circulate around the pudding.

Baked puddings have their devotees. Their texture is heavier. They should complement light meals and be served in the winter. Any pudding is made better by the addition of flaming liqueur at the table. When flaming a liqueur, use a small saucepan with a spout. Warm the liqueur or brandy for a moment, then ignite. Allow to burn until the flame subsides to take away the raw alcohol taste. Then pour over the pudding.

Steamed Chocolate Pudding

Remove the crust from:

> 8 slices of white bread

Dry in a very low oven until they break to the touch.
Meanwhile in a saucepan scald:

> 1 cup milk

Add:

> 3 ounces semisweet chocolate
> 2 tablespoons sweet butter
> ⅛ teaspoon salt

Stir until the chocolate is melted. Do not cool.
Place the bread in a large bowl; break it up coarsely. Add:

> 1 cup well-packed brown sugar
> 15 glacé cherries
> 6 egg yolks
> ½ cup rum
> 1 teaspoon vanilla
> ½ teaspoon cinnamon

Pour the hot liquid chocolate over the bread mixture and mash with a fork
or a potato masher until smooth. Beat:

> 7 egg whites

until they hold glossy peaks. Fold into the pudding mixture. Pour in
buttered mold. Cover. Cook 2 hours over low heat according to general
directions above. Watch water level and add more when necessary.

Steamed Chocolate Date Pudding

A variation of Steamed Chocolate Pudding.

Make Steamed Chocolate Pudding, above, but replace glacé cherries with:

> 1 cup chopped dates

Add to flavoring:

> 1 tablespoon frozen orange juice
> 1 tablespoon grated orange rind

Replace rum with Grand Marnier. Serve with:

> Orange Cinnamon Flavored Sour Cream,
> **page 133**

Viennese Royal Pudding

A variation of Steamed Chocolate Pudding.

Preheat oven to 225°. Make:

> 1 cup of soft pumpernickel bread crumbs

and toast on a baking sheet with:

> 4 tablespoons sweet butter

Beat:

> 8 egg yolks
> ½ cup granulated sugar

until they are light and foamy and fold in:

> 1 teaspoon grated orange peel
> ¾ cup ground unblanched almonds
> ½ cup grated sweet chocolate

Beat until they hold soft glossy peaks:

> 8 egg whites

Fold them into the batter. Fold the toasted crumbs into the pudding mixture. Pour into a well-buttered mold and cover the mold.
Steam the pudding 2 hours according to directions, page 118.
Serve with:

> Chocolate-Flecked Hard Sauce, **page 131**

VARIATION:

Add:

> ½ cup dried coconut flakes

Devil's Food Pudding

Preheat oven to 325°. Grate:

>3 ounces unsweetened chocolate

in a large saucepan over medium heat. Scald:

>½ cup milk

Add the grated chocolate and:

>½ cup granulated sugar

Cook until all ingredients are dissolved and thick, stirring constantly.
In a bowl, cream together:

>1 stick softened sweet butter
>1 cup granulated sugar
>2 egg yolks

Sift:

>2 cups cake flour
>½ teaspoon salt
>1 teaspoon baking soda

Add alternately with the dry ingredients to the butter and egg mixture:

>1 cup milk

Fold in the chocolate mixture. Beat:

>3 egg whites

until they hold glossy peaks. Fold into the batter.
Pour into a greased 8×12-inch pyrex pan and bake for 1 hour.
Serve with:

>Raspberry Sour Cream Combination, page 133

Creole Chocolate Pudding

Preheat oven to 350°. Warm a bowl. In it cream together:

>¼ cup sweet butter
>½ cup brown sugar, well packed
>2 teaspoons vanilla

Beat until fluffy. Add:

> **6 egg yolks**

one at a time, beating well after each addition. Melt:

> **4 ounces unsweetened chocolate**

over hot, but not boiling, water. Add it to the creamed mixture. Sift:

> **2 tablespoons cake flour**
> **3 tablespoons arrowroot or cornstarch**

over the mixture. Beat:

> **5 egg whites**

until they hold glossy peaks. Fold in the egg whites. Butter and flour a kugelhopf mold and fill it with the pudding mixture. Set the mold in a large pan. Pour one inch hot water into the pan. Bake 45 minutes. Let the pudding stand for 10 to 15 minutes before unmolding it on a serving dish. Sprinkle with:

> **⅔ cup chopped cashew nuts**

Serve warm with:

> **Chocolate Sauce, page 127**

Sometimes flamed with:

> **rum or Grand Marnier**

Kanonga

My grandmother's Flemish baked pudding.

Preheat oven to 350°.
Cream together:

> **4 egg yolks**
> **2 sticks sweet butter**
> **1 cup granulated sugar**

Over low heat, melt:

> **3 ounces semisweet chocolate in**
> **¼ cup water**

stirring constantly. Blend into the above mixture.

Beat:

4 egg whites

until they hold glossy peaks and fold them into the chocolate batter.

Pour into a well-buttered kugelhopf mold and place in a deep pan with water. Bake uncovered for two hours.

Cool pan and unmold only when the pudding is cold. Chill and serve with:

Eggnog Sauce, page 132

Délice au Chocolat

This pudding has the texture of a cake. It is large, heavy, rich, and scrumptious.

Preheat oven to 375°. Combine:

2 cups milk
1½ cups granulated sugar
1 stick sweet butter
8 ounces unsweetened chocolate

Bring to the boiling point over medium heat. Cool slightly.
Beat in:

4 egg yolks

Sift in:

2⅓ cups cake flour
2 teaspoons double-acting baking powder

Beat for 2 minutes with electric beater at medium speed. Beat:

4 egg whites

until they hold glossy peaks. Add them to the mixture, then pour into a 2-quart buttered mold. Bake in a pan of hot water for 1 hour. The center need not be firm, but creamy. Cool. Cut in half horizontally. Top one half with the following.

Cream:

½ cup butter

and gradually work in:

1 cup praline powder, page 194
¼ cup superfine granulated sugar

Beat until light colored.
Decorate with:

>   1½ cups toasted almonds, halved

Inca Pudding

Preheat oven to 300°.
Remove the crusts from:

>   4 slices of white bread

Dry in a very low oven until they break to the touch.
In a saucepan melt:

>   3 ounces unsweetened chocolate in
>   1 cup hot milk
>   ¾ cup granulated sugar

stirring constantly.
Add:

>   4 tablespoons sweet butter
>   1 teaspoon vanilla

Break the bread up coarsely.
Flavor with:

>   ¼ teaspoon cinnamon
>   1 tablespoon grated orange peel

Put the chocolate mixture in the blender. Add:

>   1 cup warm milk
>   2 eggs

Blend 10 seconds at medium speed. Pour into a buttered quart-size pyrex baking dish. Bake uncovered 1 hour. Serve with:

>   **Orange Cinnamon Flavored Sour Cream,**
>   page 133

Chocolate Coconut Meringue Pudding

Preheat oven to 325°. Melt:

> 2 ounces unsweetened chocolate

in foil over the pilot light of the stove. In a large saucepan scald:

> 3 cups milk

Measure:

> 2¾ cups of this milk

and in a large bowl combine with:

> 2 tablespoons sweet butter
> 8 Holland Rusks

or:

> 8 slices crusted, toasted white bread

Reserve. Dissolve:

> ½ cup well-packed brown sugar

in the remaining hot milk. Add the melted chocolate.
Combine:

> 1 cup dried coconut flakes
> ½ tablespoon grated orange rind
> 2 teaspoons vanilla
> ½ teaspoon cinnamon
> ¼ cup light rum

and mix thoroughly. Add to the large bowl mixture. Combine both mixtures. Mix until smooth. Turn into a buttered quart-size baking dish. Bake uncovered 45 minutes or until cake tester comes out clean. Top with a meringue made from:

> 2 egg whites
> ⅛ teaspoon salt
> ½ teaspoon vanilla

beaten together until they hold glossy peaks, gradually adding:

> 4 tablespoons granulated sugar

Bake again 15 minutes or until golden. Serve warm.
Orange Sauce, page 127, is good with this pudding.

Sauces for
Chocolate Recipes

Some fruit sauces combine beautifully with chocolate desserts. They are good with steamed or baked puddings, over chocolate ice creams, with chocolate soufflés, over freshly baked squares, and over pound cake.

Apricot Sauce

Soak for several hours in 1½ cups water:

> **½ pound dried apricots**

Bring to a boil and simmer until they are soft. Put in the blender or rub through a sieve with:

> **½ cup confectioners' sugar**
> **½ cup light rum**

Bring to a boil, stirring to dissolve sugar. Serve hot or chilled. Makes 2 cups.

Cherry, Raspberry, or Orange Sauce

Combine:

> 3 cups of fruit

Rub through a sieve to make 2 cups of fruit purée.
Boil together for 5 minutes:

> ½ cup sugar
> ½ cup water

Combine the purée with the syrup and flavor with:

> 2 tablespoons Cherry Heering for cherries
> 2 tablespoons Cointreau, triple sec, or
>   Curaçao for raspberries and oranges

Makes 2 cups.

Chocolate Sauce

Resembles chocolate syrup.

Melt:

> 3 ounces unsweetened chocolate

over hot, but not boiling, water. Add slowly:

> ¼ cup water

Stir until smooth. Add:

> 1 cup granulated sugar
> ½ cup light corn syrup

Boil until it reaches 238° on a candy thermometer, or soft ball stage. Remove from the heat. Add slowly:

> 1 cup evaporated milk
> 1 teaspoon vanilla

Cool thoroughly. May be stored in a covered jar in the refrigerator. Makes 2 cups.

Rum Chocolate Sauce

Over low heat melt:

6 ounces semisweet chocolate

with:

½ cup water

Stir until smooth.
Add:

½ cup granulated sugar
¼ cup white corn syrup

Boil over high heat until the mixture reaches the soft ball stage, 238° on a candy thermometer. Add:

½ cup light cream

Remove from the heat. Warm, then ignite:

¼ cup rum

Add to the sauce when the flames subside. Keep the sauce lukewarm over warm water.

VARIATIONS:

Instead of rum, use same quantity of:

Grand Marnier for orange flavor
Kahlua for coffee flavor
Cherry Heering for cherry flavor
White crème de menthe for mint flavor

Makes 2 cups.

Chocolate Fudge Sauce

In a saucepan over hot, but not boiling, water, melt:

2 ounces unsweetened chocolate

Stir in:

2 tablespoons sweet butter
2 tablespoons corn syrup

> ½ cup boiling water
> 1 cup granulated sugar
> ⅛ teaspoon salt

Continuing to stir, place the saucepan over direct heat, bring to a boil and let boil 3 minutes. Add:

> ½ teaspoon vanilla

Serve hot or cold. Makes 1½ cups.

Quick Chocolate Caramel Sauce

In a saucepan over hot, but not boiling, water combine:

> ½ cup chocolate flavored syrup
> 3 tablespoons milk
> 20 light caramels

Stir until melted.
Blend in:

> 2 tablespoons sweet butter

Serve warm. Makes 1¼ cups sauce.

Chocolate Honey Sauce

In the top of a double boiler combine:

> 6 ounces semisweet chocolate pieces
> ½ cup honey
> ¼ cup Grand Marnier
> 1 tablespoon sweet butter
> dash of salt
> 1 teaspoon orange flavoring

Heat and stir over hot, but not boiling, water until well blended. Cool. Stir in:

> ½ cup toasted slivered almonds

Makes about 1½ cups sauce. Serves 4 to 6.

Peppermint Cream Sauce

In a saucepan over hot, but not boiling, water, melt:

12 chocolate-covered mint patties

Stir in:

1 cup heavy cream

Heat the sauce to boiling point.
Add:

1 tablespoon white crème de menthe

Makes 1½ cups.

Cocoa Syrup

Over low heat, mix in a saucepan:

**1½ cups sifted confectioners' sugar
dash of salt
1 cup sifted cocoa**

Add to make a paste:

⅓ cup hot water

Then add:

⅔ cup hot water

Bring to a boil, stirring constantly. Boil 3 minutes. Stir occasionally.
Add:

2 teaspoons vanilla

Pour at once into a jar. When cool, cover and place in refrigerator.
Makes 2 cups syrup.

To make COCOA SAUCE:
Replace hot water in:

Cocoa Syrup

with:

>   1 cup hot milk

To make HONEY COCOA SAUCE:
Replace sugar in:

>   Cocoa Syrup

with:

>   same amount of honey

Rocky Road Sauce

Melt in a heavy skillet:

>   ¼ cup sweet butter

Add:

>   1 cup coarsely chopped nuts

Stir constantly, over moderate heat, till nicely browned. Remove from the heat. Add:

>   1 cup semisweet chocolate pieces

Stir until melted and smooth. Serve warm over ice cream or warm cake squares. Makes 1¼ cups.

Chocolate-Flecked Hard Sauce

Cream:

>   1 stick softened sweet butter

Gradually mix in:

>   1 egg white, unbeaten
>   1½ cups confectioners' sugar
>   2 tablespoons rum, brandy, or Grand Marnier

Beat until double in bulk.
Flavor with:

>   1 teaspoon vanilla or almond extract

according to the flavor of the dessert.
Fold in:

> ½ cup grated semisweet chocolate

Put in a mound in a bowl. Chill. Garnish with almonds or glacé cherries. Serve separately in a sauce boat. It melts on hot desserts. Makes 2½ cups.

Eggnog Sauce

Scald:

> 2 cups light cream

Melt in it:

> ½ cup granulated sugar

Beat:

> 4 egg yolks with a few grains of salt
> ½ teaspoon vanilla extract

Bring just to a boil and cook over hot water, stirring constantly, not allowing mixture to boil. Remove from heat if necessary for a few seconds. When sauce is thick enough to coat a spoon, flavor with:

> 2 tablespoons bourbon

Serve warm.
Makes 2½ cups.

Whipped Cream Combinations

To 1 cup whipped cream add:
Chantilly:

> 2 tablespoons confectioners' sugar
> 1 teaspoon of the pulp scraped from a
> vanilla bean

Amandine for chocolate:

> 1 teaspoon almond extract

      1 teaspoon orange extract
      2 tablespoons shredded toasted blanched
         almonds

Chocolate-flecked:

      ½ cup grated semisweet chocolate
      ½ teaspoon cinnamon

Sour Cream Combinations

To 1 cup sour cream, stir in to blend:
Orange cinnamon:

      ½ teaspoon cinnamon
      ½ cup orange marmalade

Raspberry:

      1 cup sieved (to remove the seeds)
         raspberry jam

Custards, Crèmes, and Mousses

Because these desserts are delicately flavored and cooked only a very short time, it is important that all ingredients be of the finest quality. Crèmes never have eggs. Crèmes with eggs are custards.

When you buy eggs for custards, remember that size has nothing to do with quality. Use medium eggs; look for grade AA or fresh-fancy. Be careful when separating the egg yolks from the whites. The thick white cordlike chalaza of the egg is a normal part of it, but it may harden in hot milk. Always remove it from egg yolks. To be sure that egg yolks do not boil in the custard and separate into minute grains of hard-cooked yolk, always break eggs into a bowl and put in about 2 tablespoons of the crème mixture to dilute them. Always add all the dry ingredients to the egg yolks; when you stir in the eggs, you automatically lower the crème temperature, which ensures smoothness and thickening.

For stirring, use only wooden spoons or whisks reserved for dessert use and rinsed in clear hot water. Wood retains odors. Onions and scented soap powders should not flavor custards or crèmes.

When adding beaten egg whites to custards, beat them until they are very stiff, since there will be no cooking heat for further expansion.

Heavy cream when whipped doubles its measurements.

Crèmes, custards, and mousses are also used as pie fillings. See page 108.

Chocolate Flan

Preheat oven to 300°. Over low heat melt and stir in:

> ½ cup water
> 8 ounces grated sweet chocolate

until the mixture is smooth.
Combine with:

> 2½ cups half and half

over high heat, uncovered. Cool it slightly and add:

> 2 teaspoons vanilla

Beat:

> 4 eggs plus 2 egg yolks

with:

> ½ cup brown sugar, well packed

until thick and foamy. Pour the mixture into a quart buttered mold. Set the dish in a pan of hot water, cover, and bake 40 minutes or until the flan is set and a knife inserted near the center comes out clean. Chill, loosen it from the sides of the dish with a knife, and unmold on a serving dish.

VARIATION:

Chocolate Caramel Flan

Dissolve, in a heavy saucepan:

> 1 cup granulated sugar
> ½ cup hot water

Boil over high heat, uncovered, until the liquid is the color of maple sugar. Remove from the heat but let the caramel darken a little more.
Have ready a chilled quart mold.
With an oven mitt, pour the caramel immediately into the mold and swirl it around to coat it. The coating hardens almost immediately.
Pour in unbaked flan mixture, above. Bake as directed above. Chill and unmold. The caramel coats the flan but "weeps" enough to make its own sauce around the flan.

Soft Chocolate Custard

This way of making the pudding prevents the formation of a "skin" on top of it.

Combine in a saucepan:

> ⅔ cup instant chocolate mix
> ⅓ cup sugar
> 3 tablespoons cornstarch
> ½ teaspoon salt

Gradually blend in:

> 3 cups milk

Cook over medium heat, stirring constantly until mixture boils.
Reduce the heat. Boil 1 minute, stirring constantly.
Remove from heat. Slowly stir about half of the chocolate mixture into:

> 3 egg yolks, slightly beaten

Add to remainder of chocolate mixture in saucepan and cook 1 minute, stirring constantly.
Remove from heat. Blend in:

> 2 tablespoons salted butter
> 1½ teaspoons vanilla

Pour into bowl and press plastic wrap directly onto pudding. Cool 15 to 20 minutes. Spoon into serving dishes. Chill. 6 servings.

VARIATION:

Chocolate Coconut Pudding

Spoon half of pudding into serving dishes. Layer with coconut and top with pudding. Garnish with coconut.

Shaker Flummery

This is a very delicate, very soft custard. When correctly made, the egg whites and the whipped cream should not be completely folded but should streak a little. Antique Waterford tumblers such as are used for old-fashioneds are good for individual servings of flummery. When you eat it, dip the spoon from the center to the outside.

Lightly crush:

> 1 pint fresh or frozen strawberries
> or raspberries

Dust with:

> ½ cup confectioners' sugar

Marinate in:

> ½ cup crème de cacao

Meanwhile, make:

> 1 recipe Soft Chocolate Custard, page 136

Cool. Beat:

> 3 egg whites

until they hold glossy peaks.
Beat:

> ½ cup heavy cream

Fold alternately the whites and half of the whipped cream into the soft custard. Pour into 6 crystal or glass bowls. In the middle of the flummery drop the fruit with the juices. Chill. The fruit will sink. Over that hole, garnish with a dollop of remaining whipped cream.

Rum Chipolata

A custard with egg white.

In a saucepan place:

> 3½ cups milk
> ½ cup granulated sugar

Bring to a boil over high heat. Meanwhile mix:

> **6 well-beaten egg yolks**
> **½ cup milk**
> **¼ cup rum**
> **1 tablespoon cornstarch**

As soon as the milk begins to boil, pour in the yolk mixture, stirring rapidly with a whisk, and remove from the heat before it boils again. It should be thick enough to coat a spoon. Cool. Meanwhile beat:

> **6 egg whites**

until stiff. Fold them into the cooled custard.
Line a 1½-quart crystal or glass bowl with:

> **about 12 ladyfingers**

Sprinkle them with:

> **½ cup tea**

mixed with:

> **½ cup rum**

Pour the custard in carefully. When cold and just before serving, garnish with an abundance of chocolate curls, page 8. Makes 6 servings.

Aga Khan III's Favorite Custard

The day before, beat together until light and foamy:

> **3 egg yolks**
> **4 tablespoons granulated sugar**

Reserve. In top of double boiler, bring to a boil:

> **1½ cups half and half**

Place the pot over simmering water. Add the reserved mixture, beating with a whisk. Add:

> **2 tablespoons Cognac**
> **⅛ teaspoon salt**

Continue to beat until the mixture thickens. Cool. Beat:

> **3 egg whites**

until stiff. Fold into the cooled sauce. Chill overnight.
Just before serving, melt in a small saucepan over hot, but not boiling, water:

> **2 packages Swiss dark chocolate**
> **(approximately 4 ounces) in**
> **½ cup milk**

In a larger saucepan, melt over medium heat:

> **2 tablespoons salted butter**

Add all at once:

> **1 tablespoon flour**

stirring with a whisk.
As it thickens, add gradually:

> **1 cup half and half**

When this boils, lower the heat and continue to stir, adding:

> **¼ cup granulated sugar**

Fold in chocolate mixture. Cook 8 minutes. Pour into individual bowls. Serve warm with the very cold sauce. Makes 4 servings.

Mont Blanc aux Marrons

Boil and shell:

> **2 pounds chestnuts**

Cook them in a double boiler until soft in:

> **1 quart milk**

Drain. Discard the milk. Make a syrup from:

> **1 cup water**
> **1 cup sugar**

Boil over high heat uncovered until the syrup turns faintly golden.
Cook the chestnuts in this for 1 minute. Flavor with:

> **2 teaspoons vanilla**
> **1 teaspoon almond extract**

Drain again. Dust thoroughly with:

> **½ cup grated semisweet chocolate**

Put the chestnuts through a ricer directly onto a serving platter, letting them fall into a mound. Don't touch them. Cover with:

> **1 cup whipped cream**

flavored with:

> **2 tablespoons crème de cacao**

Garnish with chocolate curls, page 8.
Makes 6 to 8 servings.

Cherry Chocolate Fool

The name of this crème comes from the French verb fouler, *which means to crush with the feet.*

The night before, or at least 3 hours before serving, pit:

> **1 cup sweet cherries, measured after pitting**

Mix with:

> **1 cup confectioners' sugar**

Chill. One hour before serving, drain and reserve the cherries.
In a chilled bowl, beat until it is doubled in bulk:

> **1½ cups heavy cream with**
> **¼ cup granulated sugar**

Reserve:

> **1 cup of the whipped cream**

for decoration. Into the 2 remaining cups fold:

> **½ cup instant chocolate mix**

Then fold the cherries into the chocolate flavored whipped cream. Place in a crystal or glass serving bowl. Garnish with big rosettes made from the reserved whipped cream. Chill. Serves 6 to 8.

Gelatin Chocolate Desserts

Unflavored gelatin, the best to use because it can be combined with real flavoring, comes in granular form in packets of 1 tablespoon. One tablespoon will jell 2 cups of liquid or 2⅓ cups of custard or creams. Raw pineapple or pineapple juice will not jell. It must be precooked. At least 4 hours of chilling are recommended for any dessert with gelatin. If recipes are doubled, double the chilling time and reduce the liquid by about 3 tablespoons. Gelatin used in an electric blender need not be softened. For any other recipe, gelatin should be made according to the directions on the package. Do not disturb the gelatin for 3 minutes while it softens. Then melt in the hot (75°) liquids, making sure that all crystals are dissolved by checking the bottom-most part with a spoon. Crystals, if not melted, will sink to the bottom of the mold and are the major cause of failure.

Molds should always be rinsed with cold water. For molded cream and gelatin mixtures the molds should be oiled with any unflavored vegetable oil such as peanut, corn, or walnut oil. This is done by soaking a paper towel in the oil and going over the surface and well into the decorative designs.

To unmold, rub a chilled serving platter with a wet paper towel, which makes it easier to center the mold. Insert a thin knife at four points of the edges of the mold to release the air bubbles. Place reversed mold on the dish. Place a bath towel rinsed in hot water over the mold for a few seconds. Brace the mold, holding it with the thumbs. While your fingers are under the serving plate, give one good quick shake to release the dessert. Then guide it while still covered to the exact center of the plate. Then remove the mold.

Serve on chilled platters. Place the platter over cracked ice to prevent "weeping" if served on a buffet table.

Chocolate Flummery

Marinate:

½ cup chopped candied fruit

in:

½ cup Cognac

Soften:

1 envelope unflavored gelatin

in:

¼ cup water

Meanwhile, bring to a boil:

> 1½ cups milk

Dissolve:

> ¼ cup cornstarch in
> ½ cup cold milk

Add, stirring rapidly with a whisk, to the hot milk.
As soon as it begins to thicken, reduce the heat and add:

> 1 cup granulated sugar

Continue to cook, stirring until dissolved, with:

> ½ cup grated semisweet chocolate

and the softened gelatin. Cool. Stir in the marinated candied fruit.
Beat:

> 4 egg whites

until stiff.
Rinse a pudding mold with cold water. Pour the custard into it. Cover, and chill over cracked ice in the refrigerator. Do not freeze. Unmold. Garnish with:

> Bar le Duc or currant jelly
> dollops of whipped cream

Serves 6.

Molded French Chocolate Custard

Soak:

> 1½ tablespoons gelatin in
> ¼ cup cold water

In the top of a double boiler, scald:

> 2 cups light cream

and in it dissolve:

> 1 package French or Swiss dark chocolate
> (approximately 2 ounces)

Stir in softened gelatin until all crystals are dissolved. Cool.

Beat:

> **6 egg yolks**

gradually adding:

> **¼ cup cocoa**
> **½ cup granulated sugar**

and continue until thick and foamy.
Stir in:

> **2 teaspoons vanilla**

Beat:

> **6 egg whites**

until they hold a glossy peak. Fold into the cooled chocolate mixture. Pour into a rinsed quart mold. Chill overnight. Unmold on a serving dish. Surround with:

> **Orange Cinnamon Sour Cream, page 133**

Makes 6 to 8 servings.

Minted Chocolate Rice Ring

Start one day ahead.

In the top of a double boiler, bring to a boil:

> **2 cups milk**

with:

> **¾ cup rice**
> **½ cup granulated sugar**

Stir constantly. Remove from heat and place over the bottom part of a double boiler containing simmering water. Cook for 1½ hours, stirring occasionally, replacing simmering water when needed.
Soften:

> **1 envelope unflavored gelatin**

in:

> **¼ cup cold water**

Add to rice mixture with:

> **¼ cup heavy cream**

Stir three minutes to melt the gelatin. Rinse a two-quart ring mold with cold water. Pour the rice dessert into it and chill overnight. Next day combine and melt to a smooth consistency:

> 1 ounce semisweet chocolate pieces
> ¼ cup heavy cream
> 1 envelope unflavored gelatin
> ¼ cup white crème de menthe

Cool in the refrigerator. Meanwhile invert and unmold the rice dessert on a serving platter, and immediately, with a pastry brush, coat the rice ring with the cooled—but not set—chocolate gelatin mixture. Brush patiently, dipping repeatedly into the glaze until the rice ring is well coated on the outside and the inside ring. Serve with Peppermint Cream Sauce, page 130. Makes 6 to 8 servings.

Light Chocolate Bavarian

Blend:

> ¼ cup sugar
> 1 envelope unflavored gelatin
> ¼ teaspoon salt

In a saucepan over hot, but not boiling, water, stir into dissolved gelatin:

> 1¾ cups milk
> 6 ounces milk chocolate bars

broken in small pieces. Cook, stirring constantly until gelatin and chocolate are melted and mixture is well blended. Remove from heat. Gradually stir a small amount of mixture into:

> 3 slightly beaten egg yolks

Pour this into the saucepan. Continue stirring for 2 minutes on heat. *Do not boil.* Remove from heat. Pour into bowl and press plastic wrap directly onto the mixture to prevent skin from forming. Cool. Chill until partially set. Whip:

> ½ cup heavy cream

with:

> 1 teaspoon vanilla

until it holds in peaks. Fold into the chilled chocolate mixture. Spoon into oiled 5-cup mold or equivalent individual molds. Chill overnight. Unmold and garnish as desired. Eight servings.

VARIATION:

Dark Chocolate Bavarian

Replace chocolate bars with:

> 1 cup semisweet chocolate pieces

or:

> 8 ounces unsweetened chocolate
> 1 cup granulated sugar

Chocolate Bavarian Parfait

Sprinkle:

> 2 envelopes unflavored gelatin

over:

> ⅔ cup cold water

to soften.
In another saucepan, combine:

> 4 egg yolks
> ½ cup granulated sugar
> 2 tablespoons flour
> 2 cups milk

and stir until smooth. Cook over medium heat, stirring constantly until custard coats the spoon. Remove from heat. Stir in the gelatin mixture until dissolved, then add:

> 1 tablespoon vanilla

Divide the mixture evenly into 2 large bowls and chill until the mixtures begin to thicken. Meanwhile melt:

> 1 cup semisweet chocolate pieces

over hot, but not boiling, water. Stir the melted chocolate into one bowl of chilled custard and mix until smooth. Into other bowl, stir:

> **8 drops of yellow food coloring**

Beat:

> **4 egg whites**
> **2 tablespoons sugar**
> **⅛ teaspoon salt**

until stiff but not dry. Whip:

> **½ cup heavy cream**

until it stands in soft peaks. Fold half of whipped cream and half of egg whites into the chocolate mixture. Into yellow mixture, fold remainder of whipped cream and egg whites. Alternately spoon the chocolate and the yellow mixtures into parfait glasses. Chill overnight. Makes 10 servings.

For variation, alternately pour chocolate and yellow mixtures into a 2-quart mold and chill overnight.

Plantation Cream

Start 24 hours ahead.

Bring to a boil over high heat:

> **3 cups milk**
> **1 teaspoon salt**

Slowly stir in:

> **½ cup white hominy grits**

Reduce the heat. Cover and cook 25 minutes, stirring frequently.
Soften:

> **1 tablespoon unflavored gelatin**

in:

> **½ cup maraschino cherry juice**

In a saucepan over hot, but not boiling, water, melt:

> **3 ounces unsweetened chocolate**

To the cooked grits add:

> **1 cup granulated sugar**

and the softened gelatin. Stir until both are dissolved, then add:

> ½ cup chopped maraschino cherries,
> drained
> 1 teaspoon vanilla

Remove from heat. Cool at room temperature so as not to let the cream set. Beat:

> 1 cup heavy cream

until it holds a soft peak. Fold into the grits mixture.

Pour into a well-rinsed, wet pudding mold. Chill overnight. Just before serving, unmold and decorate with sweetened whipped cream. Garnish with whole maraschino cherries. Serves 6.

Turinois, or Torino Mold

An Italian dessert.

In a saucepan over low heat melt:

> 2 ounces sweet chocolate
> 1 teaspoon vanilla
> 1½ cups water
> ½ cup granulated sugar

Stir occasionally.
Soften:

> 1 tablespoon unflavored gelatin

in:

> ¼ cup cold water

Then melt it in the chocolate mixture until all the crystals are dissolved.
In the blender place:

> 3 cups broken-up boiled chestnuts

Pour the chocolate liquid over the chestnuts and blend to a smooth paste. Pour into an oiled loaf pan and chill overnight. Before serving, unmold; cut crosswise into thick slices. Garnish each slice with a dollop of whipped cream. Makes 6 servings.

Blanc Mange aux Amandes

The most delicate of all crèmes.

To make almond milk, pound in a mortar or blend:

> **8 ounces blanched almonds**

Gradually add:

> **¼ cup water**
> **½ cup milk**

Let stand for ½ hour. Strain through a cloth. Add:

> **¼ teaspoon bitter almond extract**

Soften:

> **1 tablespoon unflavored gelatin**

in:

> **¼ cup water**

Scald:

> **1 cup light cream**
> **½ cup granulated sugar**

Dissolve the gelatin in the hot mixture. Stir in the almond milk. Chill in a mold. Serve with:

> **Chocolate Sauce, page 127**

Makes 6 servings.

Brazilian Blanco y Negra

Soften:

> **1 tablespoon unflavored gelatin**

in:

> **¼ cup cold water**

Dissolve it in:

> **1 cup very hot milk**

Add:

> ¾ cup chocolate syrup

and stir until well blended. Chill.

Make:

> 1 recipe of Blanc Mange aux Amandes, page 148

Place a 2-quart melon mold in a basin of cracked ice coming almost to the top. Pour a 1-inch layer of chocolate gelatin and allow to set. Alternate with Blanc Mange in 1-inch layers until both recipes are used up, finishing with Blanc Mange. Serve with:

> Amandine Whipped Cream, page 132

Makes 8 to 10 servings.

Soufflé Glacé au Chocolat

This is a gelatin dessert that looks like a soufflé.

In a bowl, beat with an electric beater until the mixture is light and foamy:

> 4 eggs
> 3 egg yolks
> ¼ cup granulated sugar

Soften:

> 2 tablespoons unflavored gelatin

in:

> 2 tablespoons cold water

Melt:

> 3 ounces sweet chocolate

over hot, but not boiling, water, with:

> 2 tablespoons strong coffee

Cool. Add the chocolate and the gelatin to the eggs.
Fold in:

> ½ cup whipped cream

Butter a quart soufflé dish. Turn the cream into the dish. Cut a 3-inch strip of waxed paper equal to the circumference of the soufflé dish. Stick around the top inside edge of the buttered soufflé dish. Fasten with scotch tape. Chill in the refrigerator until set. Remove the paper collar and decorate the top of the soufflé glacé with whipped cream pressed through a pastry bag fitted with a fluted tube. Makes 6 servings.

Mousses

Chocolate Mousse

In a saucepan over hot, but not boiling, water, melt:

4 ounces semisweet chocolate

Stir in:

3 tablespoons heavy cream

Flavor with:

2 tablespoons dark rum

When the mixture is cool, fold in:

2 stiffly beaten egg whites
2 cups whipped cream

sweetened with:

½ cup confectioners' sugar

Makes 6 servings.

VARIATION:

Mousse Pralinée

Omit sugar in whipped cream but fold into it:

½ cup Poudre de Praslin, page 194

Frozen Chocolate Syrup Mousse

Whip:

>   2 cups heavy cream

Fold in:

>   ½ cup Chocolate Sauce, page 126

Beat:

>   3 egg whites
>   ¼ teaspoon salt

until stiff. Fold into the chocolate mixture. Freeze in ice cube container for 3 hours. Unmold. Cut into four cubes. Serve with:

>   cold Eggnog Sauce, page 132

or use as filling for:

>   Bombes, pages 163, 164

Makes 6 servings.

Swiss Chocolate Mousse

Melt:

>   8 ounces unsweetened chocolate

Beat:

>   6 egg yolks

until almost white and frothy, gradually adding:

>   1 cup granulated sugar
>   1 tablespoon Cherry Heering

Reserve. Beat:

>   8 egg whites

until they hold in glossy peaks, and fold into the yolks.

Beat:

2 cups heavy cream

Fold into the melted chocolate, then fold into the reserved mixture.
Into:

1 cup Swiss sour cherry jam

blend:

¼ cup Cherry Heering

Spread at the bottom of a crystal or glass serving bowl. Pour the mousse over it. Decorate with a circle of blanched almond halves. Chill overnight. Serves 10.

Brussels Mousse au Chocolat

Over hot, but not boiling, water, in the top of a double boiler, melt:

8 ounces semisweet chocolate

in:

3 tablespoons Grand Marnier

Beat:

6 egg yolks

until pale yellow and frothy (this is the important part).
Add:

1 teaspoon grated orange rind
½ cup superfine granulated sugar

Fold the yolks into the chocolate.
Then beat:

7 egg whites

until stiff. Fold into the chocolate mixture. Pour into 8 pots de crème or demitasse cups and chill overnight.

50-Calorie Chocolate Mousse

Cut in small pieces:

> 2 ounces unsweetened chocolate

Place in the blender with:

> 4 tablespoons heated light rum
> 1 tablespoon liquid sweetener

Cover and blend 40 seconds. Add:

> 3 egg yolks

and blend for another 20 seconds.
Scrape from the edges of the container and fold chocolate mixture into:

> 3 stiffly beaten egg whites

Spoon into 8 demitasse cups. Chill.

Charlottes

Charlottes are gelatin creams or mousses poured into a mold lined with cake, macaroons, or ladyfingers. Molds that have splayed sides or spring-form molds are best. They should be rinsed out with cold water and un-molded like gelatin desserts, page 140.

Raspberry Chocolate Charlotte

Two days ahead make:

> 1 Viennese Chocolate Roll, page 21

filling only with:

> 1 cup raspberry jam

and no garnishes. Roll in plastic wrap or damp towel and store overnight so it will be well flavored from the raspberries. Slice the cake. Line a 1¾-quart mold with splayed sides with the cake slices. Fill with:

> Chocolate Bavarian, pages 144, 145

Chill overnight. Unmold. Fold:

> 1 cup fresh or drained frozen
> raspberries into
> 1 cup whipped cream

Place this mixture in dollops around the Charlotte. Serves 8 to 10.

Haitian Marquise au Chocolat

Very rich Charlotte.

Dip but do not soak:

> 15 Petit Beurre biscuits

in a cold mixture made of:

> ½ cup rum
> ½ cup weak coffee

Line a buttered oblong springform pan with the biscuits, leaving space between them. Crumble into small pieces:

> 8 more biscuits

Chop:

> 1 cup maraschino cherries

and reserve both. Cream together:

> 8 tablespoons sifted confectioners' sugar
> 4 egg yolks

until frothy and light. In a double boiler melt:

8 ounces semisweet chocolate
2 tablespoons sweet butter

then beat this into the egg mixture. Beat:

4 egg whites

until stiff. Fold into the chocolate mixture with the reserved biscuit crumbs and half of the cherries. Pour into the biscuit lined pan. Chill overnight. Unmold on serving platter. Ice with:

Cocoa Fudge Frosting, page 65

Decorate with silver nonpareils and chocolate curls, page 8, and the rest of the maraschino cherries. Chill until serving time. Six to 8 servings.

Low Calorie Charlotte

Place in a small deep mixing bowl:

1 package chocolate chiffon pie filling

Bring to a boil:

¾ cup milk
¼ cup strong coffee

Pour into mixing bowl and beat vigorously with a rotary beater or at highest speed of an electric mixer until filling stands in peaks (3 to 6 minutes). Add:

¼ cup granulated sugar

Beat one minute more, then add:

1 teaspoon vanilla

Break enough angel food cake into chunks to fill half a 10-inch angel cake pan with a removable bottom. Sprinkle with a mixture made from:

¼ cup blazed dark rum
½ cup coffee

Stir chunks of cake so they absorb all liquid, then fold in the filling and smooth the top of the mixture. Chill about 2 hours. To unmold, run the blade of a knife around the outside and center tube of the pan to detach the cake, turn out on a serving platter, and sprinkle lightly with:

½ cup coconut flakes

Makes 8 servings.

Soufflés and Omelettes

Omelettes should be served in individual portions. They should be made just before serving. The secrets of making soufflés are

1) to lose no time between the folding in of the egg whites and the baking;
2) not to overheat the oven;
3) to use only grade AA or fancy eggs.

Chocolate soufflés are based on a cream sauce. For best results use straight-sided ovenware soufflé dishes. Grease the bottom and sides well, and dust with a mixture of flour and confectioners' sugar. Fill ⅔ full with soufflé batter.

French soufflés are generally cooked less than American-type soufflés, 25 to 30 minutes at 350° for a quart size. Their centers remain creamy rather than dry—they develop a semisoft crust inside the soufflé dish.

American soufflés are cooked longer, 40 to 45 minutes, sitting in a pan of hot water so that no crust will form around the sides. They are less fragile. One more American trick is to fold into the batter 2 tablespoons instant tapioca.

All soufflés must be baked in the bottom ⅔ of the oven. The top unit of an electric oven must be removed. A soufflé will hold 8 extra minutes in the oven without falling. It is better to keep the guests waiting than the soufflé.

Almond Chocolate Soufflé

Preheat oven to 350°.
Beat:

> 4 egg yolks

until frothy and light. Gradually add:

> ½ cup granulated sugar
> 1 teaspoon almond extract

Reserve.
In a saucepan, over low heat, stir very rapidly with a whisk until smooth:

> 4 tablespoons melted butter
> 3 tablespoons all-purpose flour
> 3 ounces grated semisweet chocolate
> 3 tablespoons almonds, grated to a fine powder

Continue to stir rapidly, and gradually add:

> 1 cup lukewarm milk

as the mixture thickens and comes to a boil. Boil 4 minutes. Pour this mixture into the egg yolks and mix to blend. Cool over cracked ice. Beat:

> 4 egg whites

until they hold a glossy peak. Fold into the cooled mixture. Pour into a well-buttered soufflé dish. Choose French or American method, page 156, to bake the soufflé. Makes 4 servings.

Cocoa Soufflé

Lighter in color than a chocolate one.

Preheat oven to 350°.
Beat:

> 4 egg yolks

until frothy and light. Gradually add:

> ½ cup granulated sugar
> 1 teaspoon vanilla

In a saucepan over low heat, stirring with a whisk until smooth, combine:

>4 tablespoons melted salted butter
>3 tablespoons all-purpose flour
>⅓ cup cocoa
>¼ teaspoon salt

Continue to stir rapidly, and slowly add:

>1 cup lukewarm milk

as the mixture thickens and comes to a boil. Boil 4 minutes. Pour this cocoa mixture into the egg yolks and mix to blend. Cool over cracked ice. Beat:

>4 egg whites

until they hold a glossy peak and fold them into the cooled mixture. Pour into a well-buttered soufflé dish. Choose French or American method, page 156, to bake. Makes 4 servings.

Try Cinnamon-Flavored Sour Cream, page 133, on this one.

Coconut Soufflé with Chocolate Sauce

Preheat oven to 350°.
Beat:

>4 egg yolks

until frothy and light, gradually adding:

>½ cup granulated sugar
>1 teaspoon vanilla

In a saucepan combine:

>3 tablespoons melted butter

with:

>4 tablespoons flour
>¼ teaspoon salt

Gradually pour in:

>1 cup lukewarm milk

stirring very rapidly with a whisk while the mixture comes to a boil. Boil for 4 minutes. Fold the mixture into the egg yolks. Cool over cracked ice. Beat:

>4 egg whites

until they hold glossy peaks, and fold them into the yolk mixture with:

> 1 cup dried coconut flakes

Pour into a well-buttered soufflé dish. Sprinkle with an extra:

> ¼ cup dried coconut
> ⅓ cup grated semisweet chocolate

Choose French or American method, page 156, to bake. Makes 4 servings. Serve with:

> Chocolate Sauce, page 127

Chafing Dish Timbale

A clever host can make this at the table. A timbale is a soufflé made without flour. Egg whites should be beaten to the soft peak only for more rising.

In the blazer pan of a chafing dish, soften:

> 2 ounces semisweet chocolate

with:

> ¾ cup scalded heavy cream
> ¼ cup Cherry Heering

Beat until creamy with a whisk. Add:

> 3 tablespoons granulated sugar
> ⅛ teaspoon salt
> 1 teaspoon cinnamon

In separate bowls beat:

> 3 egg yolks

until light and fluffy,

> 3 egg whites

until they hold soft peaks.
First fold the yolks into the chocolate mixture, then the whites. Place boiling water in the pan under the blazer. Cover and cook the timbale over simmering water for 20 minutes without removing the cover. Spoon into serving bowls. Makes 2 servings.

Sarah McCuish Double Boiler Chocolate Soufflé

A cross between a soufflé and a timbale.

Over low heat melt:

¼ cup salted butter

in top of a double boiler. The water in the lower part should be boiling and touch the bottom of upper pan. Add:

3 tablespoons flour

and mix to blend. Gradually add:

1 cup half and half
¼ cup granulated sugar

stirring constantly. Beat:

4 egg yolks

and add to the mixture, continuing to stir until it thickens to the consistency of whipped cream. Add:

6 ounces grated semisweet chocolate
1 teaspoon vanilla

Beat:

4 egg whites

until they hold in soft peaks. Fold into the hot mixture.
Quickly cover the pan. Cook for 1 hour over low heat, adding water to the lower part of the double boiler when necessary. Serve hot with a scoop of vanilla ice cream. Makes 4 servings.

Crêpes Soufflées

Preheat oven to 375°.
Sift together:

⅔ cup all-purpose flour
¼ cup cocoa

>   1 tablespoon granulated sugar
>   ⅛ teaspoon salt

Beat until foamy:

>   2 eggs
>   2 egg yolks

Add:

>   1¾ cups milk
>   2 tablespoons melted salted butter
>   1 tablespoon brandy

Gradually add dry ingredients, beating until well blended.
Chill batter 2 hours.
Heat a 6-inch skillet and coat with sweet butter. Pour in about 2 table-spoons of the batter, rolling the pan to spread it over the entire surface. Let the crêpe brown on one side over high heat. Then with a large spatula turn the crêpe and brown the other side. Repeat, buttering the pan each time. Fold each crêpe in half.
Between the halves place:

>   ⅓ cup Cocoa Soufflé batter, page 157

for each crêpe. Glaze the top of each crêpe with apricot jam. Place crêpes next to each other in shallow baking pan. Bake 12 minutes or until well puffed. Served with Apricot Sauce, page 126. Makes 8 crêpes.

Omelette George Sand

George Sand was the pseudonym of a nineteenth-century French writer.

Heat:

>   2 tablespoons cream
>   2 tablespoons granulated sugar
>   1 ounce semisweet chocolate

in a small saucepan, stirring constantly until the chocolate is well mixed and looks like a sauce.
Beat:

>   1 egg yolk

Fold half the chocolate sauce into the beaten egg yolk, then fold in:

>   1 beaten egg white

Melt:

1 tablespoon butter

in a 5-inch frying pan over medium heat. Pour in the omelette batter. With a spoon, gently draw in the edges of the omelette, allowing the uncooked portion to flow to the edge. When set at bottom, but still creamy on top, remove from the heat. Fold over in half. Tip onto a heated serving plate. Pour the remaining half of the chocolate sauce over the omelette. Sprinkle with:

¼ cup Poudre de Praslin, page 194

One serving.

VARIATION:

Omelette George Washington

Fold:

4 tablespoons cherry preserves

into the omelette with the melted chocolate sauce. Omit Poudre de Praslin.

Frozen Desserts

Bombes glacées are the aristocrats of frozen desserts. Like many "haute cuisine" dishes, they require equipment, skill, and time. The result is, however, superb, and you may be tempted to take the trouble.

Bombes are usually made in fancy conical molds, but a pudding mold will do. Place the mold in cracked ice. Line with one mixture and fill with another to contrast the textures.

Diorama

Made by the chef of Maxim's for Christian Dior.

Line bombe with vanilla ice cream. Fill with orange sherbet. Freeze. Unmold; cover the top with as many chocolate curls as it will hold. Stack more chocolate curls like a fence around the bottom of the bombe, leaving a 2-inch space where the vanilla shows. Decorate this strip by pressing into it crystallized violets, page 200, and silver nonpareils. Serve with cold Orange Sauce, page 127.

Pâte à Bombe au Chocolat

Beat:

4 egg yolks

until thick and light. Reserve. Make:

1 recipe Italian Meringue, page 59

In a saucepan over hot, but not boiling, water, melt:

6 ounces semisweet chocolate

with:

4 tablespoons double-strength coffee

Pour the egg yolks into the meringue, beating until the mixture is very stiff, replacing the beaters with a spoon when necessary.
Beat in:

3½ cups heavy cream

Mix in, until well blended, the melted chocolate and coffee mixture. Place in a hand or electric-powered churner. Fill the drum only ¾ full with the chosen mixture to allow for expansion while freezing. Pack well with 4 parts ice to 1 part rock salt. Churn until the paddles slow down, then stop. Open the churn, pack down the ice cream. Seal the can again and see that there is enough ice and salt around it. Insulate with newspapers and let the ice cream stand 2 to 3 hours. Then, according to the recipe, use it either to line a mold, filling with a mousse of your choice, or line mold with a frozen custard or a sherbet and fill with this recipe.
Close the mold and place in the freezer on top of other packages rather than on the shelf. Remove from the freezer ½ hour before use. Unmold just before serving.

Here are classic Chocolate Bombe mixtures:

Copelia: Also called Javanaise or Danicheff bombe.
  Line with coffee or pâte à bombe ice cream. Fill with chocolate praline.
Fedora: Line with orange sherbet, fill with chocolate praline, garnish with
  canned drained mandarin orange slices and whipped cream.
Marie Louise: Line with chocolate pâte à bombe, fill with vanilla ice cream.
Nero: Line with vanilla ice cream, fill with chocolate chip ice cream.

  Unmold quickly and frost with:

1 recipe Italian Meringue, page 59

Insert half an eggshell in the top of the frosting. Fill with warm rum and ignite at the table. Pour Chocolate Sauce, page 127, around the bombe.
Alsacienne: Line with pistachio, fill with half vanilla, half chocolate pâte à bombe. Pour cold Cherry Sauce, page 127, flavored with kirsch, around the bombe.

Bombe-type desserts may be made in pudding molds using regular ice cream in the above combinations.

Frozen Chocolate Custards and Parfaits

Gelatin and custard ice creams and sherbets may be home frozen in ice cube trays with good results. Beat mixtures twice, once when they reach the mushy stage and once more before they become solid. Then cover with waxed paper to prevent ice crystals from forming.

Frozen Chocolate Custard

Mix:

> 1 cup heavy cream

into:

> 1 cooled recipe of Soft Chocolate Custard,
>   page 136

Freeze according to above directions.

Chocolate Bavarian Ice Cream

Make:

> 1 recipe Chocolate Bavarian, pages 144, 145

Pour into ice cube trays and follow above directions.

Poires Belle Hélène

Choose:

> 4 perfect ripe pears

Peel whole and leave the stems on. Cook until soft over low heat in a syrup made of:

> 1 cup water
> 1 cup granulated sugar
> 2 teaspoons vanilla

Drain. Place:

> 1 quart vanilla ice cream

in the bottom of a crystal or glass bowl.
Place the pears on top to form a cross, stems up. Fill in the spaces between them with:

> 1 cup whipped cream flavored with
> 1 teaspoon sweet vanilla

Spoon:

> a little Chocolate Sauce, page 127

over the pears to coat them. Serve the rest of the sauce from a sauce boat. Serves 4.

VARIATION:

Poires Alice

Fill an individual meringue shell with vanilla ice cream. Top with a whole pear. Dust each with:

> ¼ cup Poudre de Praslin, page 194

Glaze with:

> Chocolate Sauce, page 127

Serve additional sauce from a sauce boat.

Mole

Mole is to the Mexican what gravy is to the American. Everything can be simmered in this American Indian sauce, so old no one knows its origin.

Because wild birds and game have tougher meat than domestic animals, the original recipes invariably call for parboiling before browning the meats. With domestic birds this is now unnecessary and has been omitted from the recipes in this book.

Overnight refrigeration in mole is important for the flavor to penetrate the meats. This makes it an ideal dish for a party. Serve with green pepper and avocado salad, white or saffron rice, cornbread or tortillas which can be homemade or bought canned.

Turkey Mole or Guajalote

Select an 8- to 10-pound bird. Have it chopped into 4-inch pieces with a cleaver.
Simmer together:

> the giblets
> 2 cups of water
> 1 onion stuck with 4 whole cloves

167

Reserve. In a blender or a rotary grater or a meat grinder, grind very fine:

> 2 seeded green peppers
> 3 tablespoons sesame seeds
> ¾ cup almonds
> 3 tortillas
> 3 large seeded tomatoes
> 1½ teaspoons aniseed
> 6 cloves garlic

Season with:

> ⅛ teaspoon cloves
> ¼ teaspoon cinnamon
> 1 teaspoon salt
> ½ teaspoon nutmeg
> 2 tablespoons chili powder

Melt:

> ½ cup lard

in an earthen casserole. Stir the above mixture, which is the mole, into the fat until it is very hot. Reserve. In a heavy skillet, brown the turkey pieces in:

> **3 tablespoons lard**

Remove the pieces to the mole casserole. Cover with very hot reserved broth and simmer, covered, in 350° oven for approximately 1½ hours or until the meats are tender. Add:

> **4 ounces unsweetened chocolate**

and stir well to mix and blend. Refrigerate overnight. Reheat and serve hot. Serves 8 to 10.

Rabbit Mole: Follow the procedure for Turkey Mole.
Beef Mole: Follow the procedure for Chili Mole, below.

Chili Mole

Quickly brown:

> **2 pounds ground beef**

in:

> **1½ tablespoons lard**

Add ½ recipe mole following same procedure as for Turkey Mole, page 167.
Add before refrigerating:

2 cups cooked chili beans

Serves 4.

Crab Meat or Lobster Mole

Cook:

3 pounds shellfish

in salt water. Reserve 1 cup of the water to use instead of broth. Remove the
meat from the shells. Cut into 2-inch pieces. Use ½ of mole recipe and
follow the same procedure as for Turkey Mole, page 167. Serves 6.

Beginner's Recipes

At one time I taught a Senior Girl Scout troop how to set up, prepare, and serve a dinner from flowers to nuts. They came at 3:00 P.M. We cut the flowers and the greens from the gardens and the woods. We made a marketing list. We shopped. We cooked. When my husband came home at 7:00 P.M. he and I sat in regal splendor while the troop triumphantly brought in the fruits of their efforts, and we loved it. So did they, eating with us.

These recipes are intended for just such experiments. They are easy as well as delicious. Place emphasis on accurate measurements. Work leisurely. Have confidence.

Frozen Chocolate Drink

In a saucepan, combine:

>   2 ounces unsweetened chocolate
>   ⅓ cup sugar
>   ¼ cup dark corn syrup

Cook and stir over low heat until the chocolate is melted and the mixture is well blended. Add:

> **3 cups milk**

a small amount at a time, stirring until smooth after each addition. Stir in:

> **2 teaspoons vanilla**

Remove from heat. Pour into 9-inch square pan. Freeze about 1½ to 2 hours. The mixture will be frozen around the edges but soft in the middle. Serve in chilled parfait glasses with a straw. Garnish with whipped cream and curled chocolate, page 8. Makes 4 cups.

No-Bake Brownies

In a large bowl, combine:

> **4 cups graham cracker crumbs**
> **1 cup chopped walnuts**
> **½ cup unsifted confectioners' sugar**

Place:

> **8 ounces semisweet chocolate**
> **¾ cup evaporated milk**

in a small saucepan over low heat. Cook, stirring constantly, until the chocolate is melted and the mixture is smooth. Remove from heat. Stir in:

> **1 teaspoon vanilla**

Measure 1 cup of the chocolate mixture and set aside for glazing. Stir:

> **¼ cup evaporated milk**

into the remaining chocolate mixture. Stir into the large bowl. Spread evenly in a greased 9-inch square pan. With a spatula spread the reserved chocolate mixture over the batter. Chill. When ready to serve cut into 28 squares.

Uncooked Vanilla Fudge

In a quart saucepan melt and cook until golden brown:

> **1 stick sweet butter**

Immediately add:

>2 ounces semisweet chocolate pieces

Remove from heat, stirring rapidly until the chocolate is melted. Add:

>6 tablespoons light cream
>2 teaspoons vanilla
>⅛ teaspoon salt

Slowly stir in:

>3½ cups sifted confectioners' sugar

Pour into a greased 8×8×2-inch pan. Chill until firm enough to cut. Makes 1½ pounds candy.

Chocolate Ting-a-Lings

Melt over hot, but not boiling, water:

>12 ounces semisweet chocolate pieces

Remove from the heat and pour over:

>1 cup salted peanuts
>2 cups chow mein noodles

Toss gently until thoroughly blended. Drop from a teaspoon onto waxed paper. Chill to harden.

Choco Toast

Combine:

>2 teaspoons instant chocolate drink mix
>1 teaspoon granulated sugar

Sprinkle on hot buttered toast.
Flavor with cinnamon if desired.

Honey Chocolate Sherbet

Soften:

> 1½ teaspoons unflavored gelatin

in:

> 2 tablespoons water

Heat:

> ½ cup milk
> 2½ cups light cream
> ⅓ cup honey

until the honey is dissolved.
Add soaked gelatin, stirring until all the crystals are dissolved.
Chill. Pour in ice cube trays and freeze until mushy.
Beat with rotary beater.
Add:

> ½ cup semisweet chocolate pieces

Repeat the freezing twice more.
Serve with:

> Chocolate Honey Sauce, page 129

Chocoffee Parfait

Fill 10 parfait glasses one-third full with cold coffee.
Add:

> 2 scoops chocolate ice cream

to each glass and top with:

> about 2 cups whipped cream

Garnish with:

> chocolate curls
> glacéed cherries

Super Chocolate Freeze

Grate:

> 3 ounces sweet chocolate

Stir:

> 1 tablespoon of the grated chocolate

into:

> 1 pint softened rum raisin ice cream

Spread evenly in 2-inch square pyrex dishes. Sprinkle with:

> 1 tablespoon of the grated chocolate

Then, over this, spread:

> 1 pint softened chocolate ice cream

Sprinkle with remaining grated chocolate and:

> ½ cup toasted chopped almonds

Freeze until firm. Serves 8.

Chocolate Crescents

Buy 1 package refrigerated crescent rolls.
Preheat oven to 375°. Melt:

> 4 tablespoons sweet butter

Separate dough into 8 triangles. Brush with:

> 1 tablespoon of the melted butter

Combine:

> ¼ cup instant chocolate drink mix
> 3 tablespoons chopped pecans
> 3 tablespoons granulated sugar
> 3 tablespoons melted sweet butter
> ¼ teaspoon cinnamon

Spread each triangle with about 2 teaspoons of the mixture. Roll into crescents following package directions. Place point side down on ungreased cookie sheet. Bake 12 to 14 minutes.

Tropical Chocolate Treat

Pour into the blender:

> ½ cup chocolate flavored syrup

Add:

> 2 ripe bananas

in pieces. Blend until puréed. Add:

> 2 cups milk

Blend 10 seconds to combine ingredients. Chill.
Just before serving add:

> 2 cups vanilla ice cream, softened

Blend on medium speed for 2 seconds. If rotary beater is used, mash the bananas before mixing. Six 5-ounce servings.

Chocolate Oatmeal Crunches

Preheat oven to 375°. Cream together:

> ½ cup sweet butter or margarine
> ⅓ cup granulated sugar
> ⅓ cup brown sugar, firmly packed

Add:

> 1 egg, well beaten
> ½ teaspoon vanilla

Sift together:

> ¾ cup all-purpose flour
> ½ teaspoon salt
> 1 teaspoon baking powder

Add alternately to mixture with:

> ¼ cup milk

and blend well. Stir in:

> ½ cup chopped nuts
> 1½ cups rolled oats
> 1 cup semisweet chocolate pieces

Drop by teaspoons onto a lightly greased baking sheet. Bake 10 to 12 minutes. Makes about 4 dozen cookies.

No-Bake Cocoa Orange Balls

With a rolling pin make:

> 3 cups crumbs from vanilla wafers

Then combine with:

> 1 cup confectioners' sugar
> ¼ cup cocoa
> 1½ cups finely chopped walnuts
> 3 tablespoons corn syrup
> 6 to 8 tablespoons frozen orange juice
>   concentrate

Shape into 1-inch balls and roll in confectioners' sugar. If necessary store in airtight container and reroll in sugar before serving. Makes about 4 dozen balls.

Bananas on a Stick

Cut in halves, crosswise:

> 6 peeled, ripe bananas

Insert wooden lollipop-type stick in end of each and freeze.
In a saucepan over hot, but not boiling, water, melt:

> 1 cup semisweet chocolate pieces

Stir in:

> 1 tablespoon sweet butter

Dip and coat each frozen banana piece in the chocolate mixture. The cold will glaze the chocolate. Wrap each when dry in aluminum foil and store in freezer until ready to serve.

Fudgie Apples

Wash and dry:

> 8 to 10 medium-size apples

Insert in place of stems:

> 8 to 10 wooden lollipop sticks

In a deep, heavy saucepan, thoroughly mix:

> 2¼ cups instant chocolate drink mix
> ¼ teaspoon salt
> ½ cup evaporated milk
> 1 tablespoon cider vinegar
> 1½ cups light corn syrup

Cook over medium heat, stirring occasionally. Maintain a slow boil until the mixture reaches the soft ball stage (238°). Remove from heat and stir in:

> 1 tablespoon sweet butter
> 1 teaspoon vanilla

Keep the mixture warm while dipping the apples. Twirl apples in mixture until well coated, tipping the pan if necessary. Roll in:

> 1 cup chopped peanuts

Allow glaze to dry. Cool until ready to serve.

Bar Cake

Preheat oven to 350°. In a saucepan over hot, but not boiling, water, melt:

>5 milk chocolate bars
>½ cup chocolate-flavored syrup
>1 teaspoon vanilla

Cream until light and fluffy:

>1 cup sweet butter or margarine
>2 cups granulated sugar

Add, one at a time:

>5 eggs

beating two minutes at medium speed after each addition.
Stir together:

>¾ teaspoon baking soda
>1 cup buttermilk

Add alternately to creamed mixture with:

>2⅔ cups cake flour

Pour batter into a greased and floured 10-inch cake pan. Bake for 1 hour and 15 minutes. Allow cake to cool in the pan 10 minutes. Remove from the pan. Sprinkle with confectioners' sugar. Makes 6 to 8 servings.

Chocolate Fondue

A do-it-yourself dessert or party treat. Place a fondue pot or chafing dish of the chocolate sauce on the serving table; surround with "dippers"—fruit, cookies, mints, nuts, and such—and let everyone do his own chocolate dipping.

For two cups, combine in the fondue pan:

>2 packages semisweet chocolate
>¾ tablespoon milk
>¼ cup sugar
>¼ teaspoon cinnamon

Place over low heat and stir occasionally until chocolate is melted and mixture is perfectly smooth. Keep warm while serving. Arrange dippers on a tray or platter beside fondue; let each person dip his favorites into the chocolate. If fondue is kept warm longer than 30 minutes, add warm milk by the tablespoonful as needed to maintain proper consistency.

DIPPERS:

Seedless green grapes
Apple slices or wedges
Banana chunks or slices
Pear wedges
Stemmed cherries
Tangerine sections
Dried apricots
Prunes
Marshmallows

Dates
Candied orange rind
Butter cookies
Toasted pound cake strips
Pretzels
Rolled cookies
Ladyfingers
Flat mints

Almond Bar Pie

Preheat oven to 400°.
In a large bowl, sift together:

1¼ cups sifted all-purpose flour
⅓ cup sugar
¼ cup cocoa
½ teaspoon salt

Cut in:

½ cup shortening

until mixture looks like coarse cornmeal.
Add:

½ teaspoon vanilla

Sprinkle in:

3 to 4 tablespoons water

a tablespoonful at a time, mixing lightly until evenly moistened.
Form the dough into a ball. Chill the dough briefly before rolling.
Between two sheets of waxed paper, roll the dough into a 12-inch circle.
Remove top sheet of paper. Invert pastry onto a 9-inch pie plate.

Remove second paper and ease pastry into pie plate.
Trim dough ½ inch beyond edge of plate. Fold under and flute.
Prick bottom and sides of shell generously.
Chill 15 minutes. Bake 8 to 10 minutes.

FILLING:

Chop into small pieces:

4 milk chocolate almond bars

Melt in a saucepan over hot, but not boiling, water. Add:

**1½ cups miniature, or 15 large,
marshmallows**

Stir until dissolved. Chill thoroughly.
Whip:

1 cup whipping cream

Pour into the cooled pie shell. Chill thoroughly until firm. Top with additional sweetened whipped cream. Decorate with a sprinkling of:

¼ cup chopped toasted almonds

Candy

Successful chocolate dipping or coating depends on three things: the chocolate used, the correct temperature, and thorough stirring.

Select a room that is free of steam and cooking odors and has good air circulation, but no direct draft. Even cooling is needed for the gloss and color of chocolates. Open windows only from the top. Dip chocolates on a clear, cool day.

Dipping Chocolate

For best results, grate or chop very fine:

1 to 2 pounds semisweet chocolate

Less than 1 pound doesn't give enough depth for dipping; more than 2 pounds may cool and solidify before it can be used.

Place the top of a small double boiler containing chocolate over hot, but not boiling, water. Stir constantly with a spoon while the chocolate is melting. Be careful not to drip any water into the chocolate—moisture in the chocolate makes it unsatisfactory for dipping.

When the chocolate is completely melted, place a candy thermometer inside the double boiler. Immerse its bulb in the chocolate. Stir the chocolate with a spoon continually and rapidly, using a circular motion, until the temperature of the chocolate has reached at least 130°. Then remove the top of the double boiler from the water.

Discard the hot water at once and refill the bottom with cold tap water. Replace the chocolate and stir rapidly, scraping the sides often. Cool the chocolate evenly to 83°—the right consistency for dipping.

Remove the top of the double boiler. Quickly transfer the thermometer to the bottom part of the double boiler. Add hot water until the temperature reaches 85°; then remove the thermometer and replace the top of the double boiler. This warm water under the chocolate keeps it at the correct dipping temperature. Work rapidly while dipping chocolates because cooled chocolate stiffens suddenly.

Temperatures must be accurately controlled in all steps of dipping, particularly that of the chocolate. It affects the color and texture of the finished candy. Always use a candy thermometer and check it for accuracy each time chocolates are to be made. To check this accuracy, place it in a pan of water and bring the water to a boil. When water is boiling briskly the thermometer should register 212°. Always have the bulb of the thermometer completely immersed in the liquid and let it stand for at least one minute before reading.

OPTIMAL TEMPERATURES:

Room temperature ....60° to 70°
Water in double boiler to melt chocolate ....just below 212°
Temperature to which melted chocolate is heated.......130° to 150°
Water in double boiler to cool chocolate..............cold tap water
Water in double boiler to hold chocolate during dipping.........85°
Temperature of chocolate at which to start dipping..............83°
Temperature of chocolate to dip French creams................90°

REASONS FOR PROBLEMS:

Gray or streaked chocolates may be caused by:
    Incorrect room or chocolate temperatures
    Too much humidity
    Dipping in direct or uneven cooling
    Dipping centers that are too cold (under 70°)
    Cooling chocolates too slowly

A "foot" or broad base on chocolates occurs when dipping chocolate is too warm or excess chocolate is not removed after dipping the center. A sticky spot on chocolate may be caused by the leaking of cream centers due to incomplete coating.

Centers for dipping may be anything from an ant or a bee to a caramel. Six to seven dozen centers may be dipped from a pound of chocolate. My favorites which will keep are:

candied ginger
cherries, page 184
orange peel, page 185
whole roasted coffee beans
nut clusters
chocolate truffles, page 186
fondant, below
marzipan, page 195

Fresh fruit may be dipped but must be used the same day.

Skewer the centers on a metal knitting needle or a fondue fork. Dip the center deep in the chocolate, stirring the chocolate at the same time. Work rapidly. Drop the coated pieces on waxed paper to harden. Coffee beans can be dipped into shallow chocolate and removed with demitasse spoons. If the chocolate becomes too thick to use, scrape the sides of the pan. Melt again and resume dipping. Let freshly dipped chocolates stand for 10 minutes before moving from the paper.

Fondant

Used for cream centers and for French fondant candies.

In a large saucepan, heat, stirring constantly:

> 6 cups granulated sugar
> 2 cups cold water

When the sugar is dissolved, bring the syrup to a boil.
Add:

> 1 tablespoon corn syrup

Cook without stirring until the syrup reaches the soft ball stage, 238° on the candy thermometer. With a long fork wrapped in a damp cloth, carefully remove any sugar crystals which form on the pan. They must not fall into the syrup. Remove from the heat and cool 5 minutes. Pour onto a large rinsed but not dried platter or a marble slab. Cool to lukewarm, about 110°. Flavor small amounts with different flavorings, such as vanilla, almond, orange, strawberry, etc. Match color of flavoring with food coloring. Beat with a wooden spoon or paddle until white and creamy, and knead until very smooth.

Pack flavors separately into airtight jars and let ripen for 24 hours.

Put on a marble slab; cut into 1-inch squares or cut with candy molds. Dip in the melted chocolate.

French candymakers always dipped initials for each flavor from the tip of a spoon in a swirl on the top of each candy: V for vanilla, O for orange, etc. French creams are dipped chocolates that are rolled immediately after dipping in finely chopped nuts, candy sprinkles, or cocoa. French creams can be dipped when the melted chocolate has cooled to only 90°, since the nuts, etc., prevent the thinner chocolate from running off and forming a wide base. Fondants, undipped, make good candy when molded and glazed in the oven on a baking sheet.

The sugar in the fondant rises, crystallizes, and makes a delicious glaze. They can be decorated with silver nonpareils, candied violets, candied mimosa, etc. A truly Victorian candy.

Fondant paste may also be bought canned from bakery supply stores. It keeps a long time.

Chocolate Cherries

Select:

25 perfect fresh pitted sour cherries

Wipe each carefully with a cloth dipped in:

½ cup brandy

being careful not to break off the stem. Pack them loosely in sterile jars, stems up, and cover with the following syrup. Cook together until sugar dissolves:

3 cups granulated sugar
1 cup water

Flavor with:

½ teaspoon vanilla

Cool slightly and add:

1½ cups brandy

to the syrup. Pour this over the cherries, filling the jars to the top, and seal. Store for 6 months.

Drain the cherries well, saving the syrup for other use. Make:

1 recipe Dipping Chocolate, page 181

Dip the cherries, one by one, coating each thoroughly and forming a chocolate seal around the stem joint. Put the cherries on wax paper to harden. Store between layers of waxed paper in airtight containers.

Turtles

Melt over hot water:

8 ounces soft caramels

in:

2 tablespoons heavy cream

Cool 10 minutes. Arrange:

1 cup pecan halves

in groups of five on waxed paper (head and four legs). Spoon caramel in a small mound in the middle of the nuts to make the body. The caramel should partially cover the nuts to keep them in place. Let stand until hard. Coat body, head, and legs with dipping chocolate. Makes 18 1-inch turtles.

Orange Peel

Cutting from the navel to the stem, remove the peel from:

6 large oranges

in 3-inch strips with a sharp knife. Remove the white pulp. Bring the strips to a boil in a saucepan with enough water to cover, and cook until soft. Drain the peel on absorbent paper.

Mix:

> 3 tablespoons white corn syrup
> ½ cup water

Add the orange peel and cook over slow heat until the syrup is clear and reaches 238° on the candy thermometer. Remove peel from the syrup and drain. **Dip each strip in Dipping Chocolate, page 181. Dry on waxed paper.** Cool; store between layers of waxed paper in an airtight container.

Chocolate Truffles Duc de Praslin

In France, all dipped chocolates are called pralines. The Duke is the father of them all. The truffle is considered to be the most exquisite candy.

Melt:

> **7 ounces unsweetened chocolate**

in a double boiler with:

> **4 tablespoons sweet butter**
> **¼ cup honey**

When the mixture is soft, add:

> **1 recipe Poudre de Praslin, page 194**

Shape into uneven balls. Roll in a mixture of:

> **½ cup cocoa**
> **½ cup confectioners' sugar**
> **2 tablespoons cinnamon**

Chill until hard, then store in an airtight container.

Mexican Chocolate Truffles

Combine:

> **4 ounces grated unsweetened chocolate**
> **⅓ cup confectioners' sugar**
> **⅓ cup almond paste**

1 tablespoon double-strength warm coffee
1 teaspoon sweet butter

Mix to blend until it forms a smooth paste. Shape in 2 dozen balls ½ inch in diameter. Roll in:

¼ cup cocoa
1½ teaspoons cinnamon

mixed together. Chill before serving.

Hazelnut Truffles

The modern Parisian recipe.

In a saucepan combine:

1 cup ground hazelnuts
½ cup granulated sugar
2 ounces semisweet chocolate

Gradually add:

⅓ cup water
2 tablespoons sweet butter

Flavor with:

1 teaspoon cinnamon

Cook over very low heat, stirring constantly until the sugar is dissolved and the chocolate melted. Cool, then roll into uneven balls the size of a walnut. Spear each chocolate ball on a toothpick and coat them with Dipping Chocolate, page 181. Place them on waxed paper and harden in the refrigerator.

Brazil Truffles

These mellow truffles with a mocha taste are very special.

In a saucepan over hot, but not boiling, water, melt:

3 ounces unsweetened chocolate

with:

> ⅓ cup sweet butter
> 1¼ cups sifted confectioners' sugar
>   (no substitute)
> 2 tablespoons coffee liqueur

Mix to blend until smooth. Beat in:

> 4 egg yolks

one at a time. Chill until the mixture is stiff enough to form walnut-sized irregular balls. Roll in grated Brazil nuts. Chill.

Opera Fudge

A basic American fudge recipe, except this one is frosted.

In a heavy quart saucepan, combine:

> 2 cups granulated sugar
> ⅛ teaspoon salt
> ¾ cup heavy cream
> ½ cup milk
> 1 tablespoon white corn syrup
> 1 teaspoon vanilla
> ¾ cup chopped walnuts
> 3 ounces unsweetened chocolate

Boil over low heat, stirring constantly until the mixture reaches the soft ball stage or 238° on the candy thermometer. Remove from heat. Spread over the top:

> 6 ounces melted semisweet chocolate

Chill until the chocolate is firm. Cut into 5 dozen squares.

Vassar Fudge

Combine:

> 2 cups granulated sugar
> 2 ounces coarsely chopped unsweetened
>   chocolate

1 cup half and half

Cook over medium heat, stirring until the chocolate is melted. Continue to cook until the mixture reaches soft ball stage or 238° on the candy thermometer. Remove from heat. Add:

1 tablespoon sweet butter

without stirring. Cool until the fudge reaches 110°.
Beat with a wooden spoon until the candy loses its gloss. Transfer to a buttered plate. Cut into squares before it becomes firm.

Wellesley Fudge

Follow method for Vassar Fudge. When the fudge is removed from the heat, beat in:

8 ounces softened marshmallows

Smith Fudge

In a heavy quart saucepan, combine:

1 cup granulated sugar
1 cup brown sugar, well packed
¼ cup dark molasses
½ cup heavy cream
2 ounces coarsely chopped unsweetened chocolate

Boil over low heat, stirring constantly until the mixture reaches the soft ball stage or 238° on the candy thermometer. Remove from heat. Add:

½ stick sweet butter
1½ teaspoons vanilla

Beat with a wooden spoon until the fudge loses its gloss. Pour into a buttered 8-inch square pan. Cut immediately into 2 dozen squares.

Minted Chocolate Fudge

Bring to boiling point:

> 1 cup light cream
> 2 cups granulated sugar

Stir until the sugar is melted and reserve. In a quart bowl place:

> 4 ounces unsweetened chocolate

and cover with boiling water. Cover and leave for 5 minutes. Pour off all the water except 1 tablespoon and stir. Mix the chocolate into the cream and sugar mixture. Add:

> ¼ cup honey
> ¼ cup green crème de menthe

Cook to the soft ball stage, 238°. Add:

> 2 tablespoons sweet butter

and remove from the heat. Let stand until lukewarm, then beat until creamy. Add:

> 1 cup chopped pistachio nuts

Pour into a buttered pan and dust with approximately:

> ¼ cup blanched grated pistachio nuts

Cool. When firm, cut into 5 dozen squares.

Apricot Fudge

Mix in a heavy 2-quart saucepan:

> 1¼ cups granulated sugar
> ¼ cup sweet butter
> ¾ cup evaporated milk
> 7 ounces Almond Fluff Topping, page 73

Over high heat, bring to a bubbling boil, stirring constantly. Reduce to medium heat when bubbles appear all over the top. Stir 8 minutes. Remove from heat and add:

>2 cups milk chocolate pieces

stirring until completely melted. Add:

>1 teaspoon vanilla
>½ cup chopped walnuts
>½ cup chopped dried apricots

Pour into a greased 8- or 9-inch square pan. Cool thoroughly. Makes 3 dozen squares, or 2¼ pounds fudge.

Chocolate Almond Brittle

Combine:

>2 cups granulated sugar
>⅓ cup white corn syrup
>⅔ cup cold water
>¼ cup sweet butter

Cook and stir until the sugar is dissolved. Continue cooking without stirring to 300° on the candy thermometer. When the syrup makes hard brittle threads, remove from heat. Melt into it, stirring very rapidly:

>½ cup grated semisweet chocolate
>1 teaspoon vanilla
>½ teaspoon baking soda
>1½ cups chopped roasted almonds

Pour onto greased cookie sheet. When cool enough to handle, pull the edges to thin it and overlap it on a second greased cookie sheet. When cold, break into pieces. Makes 1½ pounds of candy

---

VARIATION:

Chocolate Peanut Brittle

Replace almonds with unsalted peanuts.

English Toffee

A two-color candy, it looks striped.

Coarsely grind:

1 cup toasted almonds

and spread in the bottom of a 7×11-inch buttered pan.
In a heavy skillet, combine:

1 cup sweet butter
1 cup granulated sugar

Cook and stir and let boil over medium heat until it reaches 300° or hard crack stage. Protecting yourself from spattering, pour at once and slowly, so the nuts don't bunch, into the buttered pan. Let stand 7 minutes, or until the top begins to set. Sprinkle:

⅓ cup grated semisweet chocolate

over the caramel in the pan. The chocolate will melt from the heat of the candy. Smooth with a spatula. Cool until you can handle it with your fingers. Cut by the teaspoonful. Shape into a toffee (oblong roll). Let harden on waxed paper. Wrap individually.

Baño

A Spanish candy.

Over low heat, melt:

3 ounces unsweetened chocolate in
1¼ cups milk

Add:

 3 cups granulated sugar
 1 tablespoon cornmeal
 ¼ teaspoon salt
 3 tablespoons sweet butter

Cook and let boil until it reaches 238° on the candy thermometer, or soft ball stage. Pour into an 8×8-inch greased pan. Cool. Cut into 2×1-inch rectangles. Lift from the pan as soon as they are cool enough to handle. Shape into little cigars. Let harden on waxed paper. Wrap individually.

Chocolate Nougat

In a quart-size saucepan, combine and cook together:

 1 cup honey
 6 tablespoons light corn syrup
 2 cups granulated sugar

until they reach 265° on the candy thermometer. Beat:

 3 egg whites

until stiff. Slowly add the syrup to the egg whites, still beating. Combine:

 1 cup cocoa

with:

 2 tablespoons water

and beat into the egg white mixture. When the mixture stiffens, add:

 1 cup coarsely chopped almonds
 ½ cup halved glacé cherries
 1 teaspoon almond extract

Line an 8×4×3-inch pan with wafer paper. (You can obtain it from a bakery supply house.) If not available, grease the pan. Pour the mixture into the pan. Cut in 2×1-inch bars before it is cold. Remove to waxed paper until cold.

Poudre de Praslin, or Praline Powder

Used as a base in many confections and some desserts.

In a quart saucepan melt:

> 2¼ cups granulated sugar in
> 1½ cups water

and allow to boil uncovered over high heat to the hard crack stage (295° on the candy thermometer). Spread:

> 1 cup blanched almonds

mixed with:

> 1 cup blanched hazelnuts

on a buttered cookie pan and pour the caramel on it. Cool. When it is hard, break with a hammer and grind to a powder in an electric blender (be sure container is dry) or crush to a powder with a rolling pin.
Praline powder for 50 confections.

Marzipan Potatoes

Pound in a mortar or blend to a fine powder:

> 4 cups chopped blanched almonds

Make a paste of this powder with:

> 4 cups packed confectioners' sugar
> 3 egg whites
> ⅓ cup sifted flour

Roll the paste into 18 to 24 balls resembling small potatoes. Pat on a marble slab. Cool. Roll the potatoes in instant chocolate drink mix until they are light brown. Store between sheets of waxed paper in an airtight container.

Marzipan Centers

Pat the marzipan above on a marble slab or a large rinsed, but not dried, platter. Divide, flavor with different extracts (almond, orange, mint, etc.) and tint with food color to match.

Cut into 1-inch squares or small rounds or fancy shapes with special candy molds. Dip according to directions for Dipping Chocolate, page 181.

Chocolate Decorations

Chocolate Leaf Decorations

Draw or trace 4 dozen ivy or maple or holly leaves on waxed paper, and cut out.

Place them on ungreased baking sheets. Carefully brush on:

> ⅛ inch layer of hot Hard Chocolate Icing,
> **page 61**

not quite to the edge of the paper leaves, so that it will be easy to remove the chocolate leaf from the paper when cold.

Chill until the leaves are firm. Store for further use between waxed paper in airtight container.

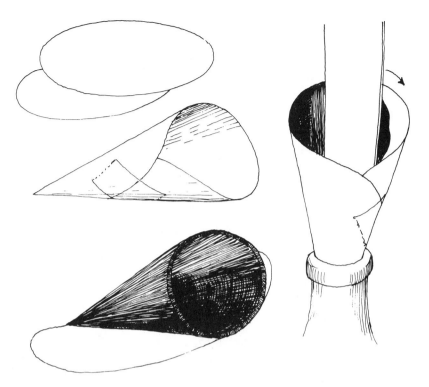

Chocolate Cornucopias

Cut 2 dozen 3-inch waxed paper circles. Form into cornucopias and fasten with Scotch tape. Put each one in the neck of an empty soda bottle. With a small spatula, coat insides with:

hot Hard Chocolate Icing, page 61

or:

8 ounces melted Swiss or French dark sweet chocolate as for Colettes, below

When cool, peel off paper and store.

Colettes

Filled chocolate cups.

In a saucepan over hot, but not boiling, water, melt:

> 2 packages dark sweet French or Swiss
> chocolate (100 grams or approximately
> 4 ounces each)

With a spoon or small spatula, coat the inside of 6 paper cupcake cups, covering the entire pleated surface and bottom with a thin layer of chocolate. Place the cups in muffin pans and chill until the coating is firm. When ready to use, peel off the paper and fill the cups with ice cream. Garnish with chopped nuts or shredded coconut and a grating of semisweet chocolate.

Marie-Josés

Named after a Belgian princess.

Follow the preceding recipe for making chocolate cups. When ready to use, place a thin layer of:

> **pound cake soaked in maraschino liquid**

in the bottom of the cup. With a pastry tube, fill the cup with a big rosette of:

> **vanilla flavored whipped cream**

and top with:

> **a maraschino cherry**

Copinhos Delicia

The Brazilian version of Marie-Josés, *the ultimate unique blend of textures and flavors.*

Half fill the chocolate cup with:

> **Crème Patissière, page 69**

Cover with:

> **Chocolate Mousse, page 150**

Top with:

> **Orange Cinnamon Sour Cream, page 133**

Schlosserbuben

A very special fritter which is called a confection in Vienna and served with coffee.

Soak overnight in dry white wine:

> **1 pound large pitted prunes**

Drain the prunes, reserving the wine, and simmer in water to cover for 30 minutes. Cool. Fill each prune with:

> **a blanched almond**

Chill thoroughly. Make a batter by combining:

> **1 cup flour**
> **1 cup of the wine in which the prunes**
> **were soaked**

Beat the batter until smooth with:

> **⅛ teaspoon salt**

Dip the prunes in the batter and fry in 390° deep fat until golden. Drain on absorbent paper and roll in:

> **1 cup grated sweet chocolate**

Serve at once.

Chocolate Strata Squares

Half cookie, half chewy candy.

Preheat oven to 350°. Melt:

> **½ cup sweet butter**

in 9-inch square pan. Tilt pan to cover the bottom completely with the butter. In layers, one after the other, sprinkle pan with:

> **1 cup graham cracker crumbs**
> **1 cup chopped nuts**
> **1 cup semisweet chocolate pieces**
> **1 cup flaked coconut**

Pour over the top:

1 can sweetened condensed milk

Do not stir. Bake 25 to 30 minutes. Cool. Cut into 3 dozen 1½-inch squares.

Crystallized Rose Petals, Violets, or Mimosa

These are imported from the South of France by gourmet sections of many department stores. But they are fun to make and keep very well in airtight containers.

Utensils needed: a round cake pan 2 inches deep, about 9 to 10 inches in diameter, and a steamer rack to fit it.

Remove the stems from:

1 pound violets, or use dark red rose petals, mimosa puffs, or lilac-colored acacia

Cook:

3 pounds granulated sugar

in:

1 quart water

until it reaches 238° or soft ball stage. Cool. Add:

2 drops essence of rose geranium, a perfume fixative available at good pharmacies

In the cake pan, pour a layer of the syrup 1 inch deep. In it place the rack. Spread the flowers on it in the syrup, adding enough cooled syrup so that they are fully covered. Reserve the rest of the syrup over the pilot light of the stove. Cover the pan with a wet towel to prevent the sugar from becoming crystallized between the flowers, and let stand for 5 hours; then add the rest of the syrup and let stand overnight covered with the wet towel. Lift the rack from the pan, set it on a tray, and let the flowers dry at room temperature. Store in airtight containers. Keep in a cabinet away from steam. Use for decorating dipped chocolate and some French cakes.

Beverages

When you can't eat chocolate, *drink it.*

Pinillo, or Champurrado

This is the original Indian chocolate food.

In the top of a quart-size double boiler, scald:

> 2 cups milk
> ½ cup heavy cream

Flavor with:

> ⅛ teaspoon salt
> ⅛ teaspoon nutmeg
> ⅛ teaspoon allspice
> 1 teaspoon cinnamon

Reserve.
Grate:

> 2 ounces unsweetened chocolate, or
> grind roasted cocoa beans

Dilute with:

> ½ cup hot water

When the chocolate is melted, beat with a molinillo or rotary beater until smooth and foamy. Add to the milk mixture and cook for 1 hour over water below the boiling point, beating from time to time.

Before serving, beat together until well mixed:

> 1 egg
> ½ teaspoon vanilla
> ½ cup of milk
> 5 tablespoons cornstarch

Pour into the double boiler mixture; stir until well mixed. Cook slowly, stirring all the time until mixture is thickened. Serve at once from Jicaras or tall porcelain cups.

Fruit Champurrado

This is a thick drink which is eaten with a spoon from wide tall glasses. Perfect for a patio evening.

Wash and drain:

> 1 pint raspberries
> 1 pint strawberries

Add:

> 3 tablespoons granulated sugar

Drain:

> 8-ounce can sliced peaches

and in the syrup bring the berries to a boil for 1 second. Chill. Mix with the sliced peaches. Spoon into 6 glasses. Pour over the fruit and syrup:

> 1 recipe chilled Pinillo, page 201

Mocha Milk Shake

Place in blender:

>3 cups milk
>⅔ cup instant chocolate drink mix
>1 teaspoon instant coffee
>2 cups coffee ice cream, softened

Blend until all ingredients are combined.
About three 12-ounce servings.

Dutch Cocoa

Mix in a saucepan with a spout:

>4 tablespoons Dutch processed cocoa
>   (no substitute)
>4 cups lukewarm water

Bring to the boiling point.
Whip:

>⅓ cup chilled heavy cream

with:

>2 teaspoons superfine granulated sugar

Pour the cocoa into a mug. Top with the whipped cream and sprinkle with:

>a grating of nutmeg or mace

to taste. Do not stir. Drink the hot cocoa through the sweet chilled cream.
Four servings.

Cinnamon Cocoa

Combine in a saucepan:

> ¼ cup cocoa
> ¼ cup granulated sugar
> ⅛ teaspoon salt

Add slowly, beating until it makes a thick paste:

> 1 cup water

Stir in:

> 3 cups milk
> 1 teaspoon vanilla
> ⅛ teaspoon cinnamon

Beat with a molinillo or rotary beater until frothy.
Makes 1 quart or 6 servings.

French Breakfast Chocolate

This is not so sweet as American chocolate and has a different texture.

Place in a saucepan:

> 6 ounces grated sweet chocolate
> ⅓ cup hot water

Over hot, but not boiling, water, melt the chocolate and beat it with a whisk until it forms a heavy paste. Thin the paste with another:

> ⅓ cup hot water

Stir and pour into large cups or mugs, filling them only half full. Fill with:

> 2 cups very hot milk

Don't mix. Two servings.

Spanish Cocoa for a Party

Stir together in a 6-quart saucepan:

>   1¼ cups cocoa
>   1½ cups sugar
>   ¾ teaspoon salt

Slowly stir in:

>   2 cups hot water

Heat gently for 2 minutes, stirring constantly. *Do not boil.* Remove from heat. Stir in:

>   1 tablespoon vanilla

Beat with a rotary beater until foamy. Serve hot. Makes 4½ quarts or 24 6-ounce servings.
Serve with a cinnamon stick in each cup.

Chocolate Eggnog

Combine in a saucepan:

>   ⅔ cup instant chocolate drink mix
>   ¼ cup sugar
>   ¼ teaspoon salt
>   2 cups milk
>   4 egg yolks, slightly beaten

Cook over medium heat, stirring constantly until mixture just coats a spoon. Chill.
Just before serving, beat together until stiff peaks form:

>   4 egg whites
>   2 tablespoons sugar

On low speed of mixer gradually blend in:

>   the egg whites
>   3 tablespoons instant chocolate drink mix
>   ¼ cup light rum

Fold into the chilled eggnog. Sprinkle with cinnamon or nutmeg. Makes 6 cups.

Café Liègeois

A popular dessert drink in the eastern part of Belgium.

In a bowl, stir to soften:

> ½ pint rich chocolate ice cream

In another bowl, stir and combine:

> 1 pint coffee ice cream
> ¼ cup Cognac

Divide the Cognac-flavored ice cream in the bottom of 4 large stemmed wine glasses. Put the chocolate ice cream on top. Chill.
Whip:

> ⅓ cup heavy cream

Top the chocolate ice cream in the glasses with a large rosette of cream. Serve immediately with short straws. Makes 3 cups.

Sazerack Club Chocolate

To:

> 1 cup hot chocolate (use directions on
> package)

add:

> 1 jigger Pernod or Riccard or ouzo

Beat with a *molinillo* or a beater. Top with a rosette of whipped cream.

Crème de Cacao

For those who have an old-fashioned druggist who carries cocoa beans.

Roast:

1 pound cocoa beans

to a light brown in an ungreased iron skillet over low heat, stirring constantly. Grind in a coffee mill.
Pour:

2 quarts good brandy

over the ground beans and let stand for 6 days.
Boil together uncovered:

2 cups granulated sugar
4 cups water

over high heat until reduced to half the quantity. Add the cacao and the brandy. Flavor with:

2 tablespoons vanilla

Drip through a coffee filter into 2 bottles and cork leftovers for further use. Makes 4 quarts.
This liqueur can be bought imported and domestic.

Café Frappé

Half fill a small cocktail shaker with:

1 cup finely shaved ice
½ cup cold double-strength coffee
½ cup crème de cacao

Shake well. Serve from champagne coupés with short straws. Two servings.

Pousse-Café

Served in France and French-speaking countries with demitasse.

In a tall fluted glass, pour slowly so they don't mix:

> 2 tablespoons grenadine
> 2 tablespoons creme de cacao
> 2 tablespoons maraschino liqueur
> 2 tablespoons orange Curaçao
> 2 tablespoons green crème de menthe
> 2 tablespoons parfait amour liqueur
> 2 tablespoons Cognac

One serving.

Low Calorie Chocolate Milk Shake

Make:

> ½ quart Spanish Cocoa, page 205

using powdered skim milk according to directions on milk package. Freeze to the mushy stage in ice trays.

In the blender combine:

> 1 cup chilled club soda
> the Spanish frozen cocoa
> 2 tablespoons commercial chocolate syrup

Blend until foamy. Each serving is 75 calories. Makes 4 cups.

Index